M000190111

CATHEDRALS OF WAR

CATHEDRALS OF WAR

Florida's Coastal Forts

MICHAEL GARLOCK

Pineapple Press
Palm Beach, Florida

 Pineapple Press

An imprint of Globe Pequot, the trade division of
The Rowman & Littlefield Publishing Group, Inc.
4501 Forbes Boulevard, Suite 200, Lanham, Maryland 20706
www.rowman.com

Distributed by NATIONAL BOOK NETWORK

Copyright © 2022 Michael Garlock

All rights reserved. No part of this book. may be reproduced in any form or by
any electronic or mechanical means, including information storage and retrieval
systems, without written permission from the publisher, except by a reviewer
who may quote passages in a review.

British Library Cataloguing in Publication Information Available

Library of Congress Cataloging-in-Publication Data

ISBN 978-1-6833-4-269-4 (paper : alk. paper)
ISBN 978-1-6833-4-270-0 (electronic)

♾™ The paper used in this publication meets the minimum requirements of
American National Standard for Information Sciences—Permanence of Paper
for Printed Library Materials, ANSI/NISO Z39.48-1992.

CONTENTS

INTRODUCTION

On the east coast in St. Augustine, the Spanish build a colossal fort while 400 miles almost due west in Pensacola already established British forts were under siege.

The genesis for the exploitative, colonialist designs on the New World had their origins centuries before the establishment of the United States and Florida. A single Spanish monarchy was established by the Catholic Monarchs Isabella of Castile, Queen of Castile, and her husband King Ferdinand, King of Aragon, when they were married in 1496, thus creating a de facto unification of Spain. Together they gave their official approval and financing to allow the Genoese mariner Christopher Columbus to try and reach India by sailing west. Funding and profits flowed to Castile while the monarchy controlled the authority for conquest, discovery, and settlement.

Financed by almost unlimited funds and a cadre of ambitious adventurers, explorers, and conquistadores, all of whom sought wealth and power beyond their wildest dreams, Spain invaded the Americas and incorporated them into the Spanish Empire with the exception of Canada, Brazil, and the northeastern United States.

The discovery of America by Columbus in 1492 was a watershed moment, and for the next 300 years the Spanish Empire would expand over the Caribbean Islands, half of South America, Mexico, and Florida. Mini armadas regularly sailed from

Spain while heavily laden galleons plowed through the ocean and returned with plunder that fattened Spain's coffers.

Columbus was given virtual carte blanche and was rewarded by governorship of the new territories and in subsequent voyages founded La Navidad on what would later be known as Hispaniola in Haiti. In 1496, his brother Bartholomew founded Santo Domingo. Sovereignty was established and large, permanent settlements were meticulously planned to replicate the finer aspects of Castilian life in the new world.

The first settlement, Santa Maria la Antigua del Darien in Castillo de Oro, was established in 1510 by Vasco Núñez de Balboa in what is what is now Colombia, Nicaragua, Panama, and Costa Rica. Balboa crossed the Isthmus of Panama and claimed all the lands adjoining the Pacific Ocean for Spain. It was the equivalent of a land rush in slow motion. More settlers eager for a new and better life willingly filled transport ships and endured weeks of cramped quarters, bad food, and often volatile weather. The increasing number of people leaving Spain meant more land had to be conquered with presumptive treasure waiting to be found. The first permanent settlement was in Hispaniola and later Cuba and Puerto Rico. All, however, was not smooth sailing.

Proactive popes were involved, as they often were in the 1480s. Pope Sixtus IV in his what was later proved to be short-sighted wisdom granted Portugal the rights for all the land south of the Cape Verde Islands. The Portuguese king, King John II to whom Columbus had initially offered his services but was not taken up on his offer by the equally shortsighted king now claimed that the lands discovered by Columbus belonged jointly to Portugal, not Spain. After years of squabbling, in 1493 two papal decrees issued by the Spanish-born Pope Alexander VI finally settled the matter. Spain's claims were unsurprisingly upheld. In a somewhat desperate attempt to save whatever he could of Portugal's holdings King Joao II negotiated a treaty with Spain.

In 1494 the Treaty of Tordesellas literally and figuratively drew a line north to south through South America. Territory west of the line belonged to Spain, while lands east of the line were Portugal's, including the east coast of Brazil, making Portuguese the official language of Brazil. Portugal was left with a miasmic sliver of predominantly jungle-filled Brazil and most of the sparsely populated, barren West Africa while Spain got all of South America and North America. Spain became a world power while Portugal resigned itself to the inevitable—not having any practical influence in world affairs.

The floodgates opened for years of relentless, systematic, ruthless, and often brutal conquests. Fantastical tales of rivers of gold (obviously not true but a powerful lure and motivator nonetheless) and semi-passive natives who posed no physical threat and therefore were incapable of putting up anything that even slightly resembled an organized resistance, enabled, and encouraged armor-wearing, horse-riding conquistadores to begin their exploitation of South America and Mexico.

In 1504 Hernán Cortés, born into a family of lesser nobility participated in the conquest of Hispaniola before he explored the Yucatán Peninsula. Still going strong 15 years later, Cortés entered the capital of the Aztec Empire with an army of 600 men whose weapons included swords and harquebuses. The gold that seemed to be everywhere fueled his desire for conquest and lined his pockets and those of his men. Breastplates and helmets provided protection against cruder Indian weapons while horses gave them a tactical and psychological advantage.

It took Cortés 11 years to fight what was basically a war of attrition, but the indefatigable Cortés dismantled and defeated the Aztecs and claimed their capital Tenochtitlan for Spain and

renamed it Mexico City. The Aztecs' skill at fashioning ear-
rings, rings, necklaces, leg bracelets, and arm bracelets from
jade, quartz, opal, turquoise, and moonstone resulted in even
the lowest-ranking conquistador sending enough gold, silver
and precious jewels home to Spain to ensure his family's future
for generations even after giving the monarchs their share. It
was no surprise that many large-scale expeditions were readily
financed and launched. The Spanish treasury bulged with newfound riches and enabled the monarchy to build more ships and
increase the size of their army.

Chief among the conquerors was Francisco Pizarro, also
born into a relatively poor family, who in 1509 made his way
to the Spanish Caribbean. From there he and his men ventured south, where he participated in successful expeditions in
Panama before being lured south by tantalizing and irresistible
rumors of Inca wealth in Peru. Unlike other rumors that sent
Spanish explorers on wild-goose chases, Peru was rich in silver
and highly toxic mercury used for separating pure silver from
silver ore.

Pizarro's first efforts in the 1520s failed, but he persevered,
executed the Inca emperor Atahualpa in 1532, and a year
later founded Lima. Like the Aztecs, the Incas had enormous
resources of silver, gold, and jewelry made of lapis lazuli.
They even mined gold. It was another bonanza waiting to be
exploited, which was exactly what happened.

Farther to the north, there was more activity. Francisco
Vasquez de Coronado went to Mexico in 1535, joining Antonio de Mendoza who had been named viceroy of the newly
founded colony known as New Spain. Their respective fathers
had been close associates in Spain. That connection and the
fortuitous marriage to a wealthy woman enabled Coronado,
upon the recommendation of Antonio Mendoza, to lead an
expedition in search of the Seven Cities of Cibola. Another

Spanish explorer, Cabeza de Vaca, had reported that these Native American cities were filled with gold.

In February 1540, leading a force of about 300 Spanish soldiers, several hundred natives and herds of horses, cattle, and other livestock, Coronado headed up the west coast of Mexico and eventually crossed into Southeast Arizona. For the next two years he explored parts of what is now Arizona, New Mexico, Kansas, Oklahoma, and Texas. He also found the untamed Colorado River and the breathtakingly beautiful and awe-inspiring Grand Canyon, but the Seven Cities of Gold proved to be just another myth. In the fall of 1542, he returned to Mexico empty-handed.

At the same time, another Spaniard, Hernando de Soto, was making inroads into what today is the southeastern United States. Involved in previous expeditions in Nicaragua and the Yucatán Peninsula he also played an important part in Pizarro's conquest of the Inca Empire. From 1539 to 1542 de Soto and his expedition explored parts of Florida, Georgia, North and South Carolina, Alabama, Mississippi, Louisiana, and Tennessee and even ventured as far west as Arkansas, Oklahoma, and Texas. He is the first European documented as having crossed the Mississippi River. After de Soto died of sickness in 1542, the surviving men returned to Mexico City empty-handed without finding the treasures of gold and silver, they were led to believe awaited them.

Despite these setbacks, the conquests of South America, Central America, and Mexico by seasoned, ambitious campaigners brought enormous wealth to Spain, glory to those who survived, and disease and destruction to the native people who opposed the Spaniards, Spain was firmly established as a world power to be reckoned with.

While conquistadores were often traveling thousands of miles on foot and horseback through hostile, unknown territory in search of gold, silver, and new land to appropriate for Spain, one explorer stayed closer to home. Juan Ponce de León first came to the Americas with Christopher Columbus's second expedition in 1493, along with 1,200 sailors, colonists, and soldiers. By 1511, rumors of undiscovered islands northwest of Hispaniola had reached Spain. Because he was instrumental in crushing a rebellion there while exploiting the indigenous tribes who mined gold, de León was given permission to make a reconnaissance to Puerto Rico, where it was rumored that fertile lands were full of gold.

The expedition was successful, and de León was made governor. However, legal wrangling over control of Hispaniola and Puerto Rico initiated by Diego Colon, son of Christopher Columbus, eventually resulted in de León being stripped of his powers. To reward de León for his faithful service and to prevent further discovery and expeditions by Colon, King Ferdinand encouraged de León to explore for undiscovered islands to the northwest of Hispaniola that were beyond the reach of Colon's authority. In exchange, de León was given exclusive rights to any land he found, along with being made governor. Naturally, profits would be shared with the monarchy, and as a further stipulation de León had to finance the expedition himself.

A HISTORY OF AMERICAN FORTS

*L*ike any fledging nation, America had to go through lengthy and tumultuous growing pains. Initially facing internal and external existential threats, the newly born country prudently established forts whose locations were specifically chosen to counteract immediate dangers.

Acting out of a defensive posture, the colonists sought to somehow maintain a toehold in the huge landmass that was to become the United States. Over the course of time, French military theorists seeing an opportunity to promulgate their ideas began to insinuate themselves into American strategic planning and thinking, but it was the colonists who pragmatically laid the initial groundwork for what was to come.

The colonial period was busy in terms of fort construction. Most were relatively unsophisticated installations that have not survived. Although predominantly situated on the east coast some were on the other side of the country and even Hawaii. Many were subsequently refurbished in the Revolutionary War, thus extending their usefulness. Here is a representative sampling.

Colonial Period Refurbished Forts

- Fort Amsterdam a.k.a. Fort George, New York City, New York
- Fort Barrancas, Pensacola, Florida. This fort later became an iconic Third System fort.
- Fort Charlotte/Fort Condé, Mobile, Alabama
- Fort Constitution, Portsmouth, New Hampshire
- Fort Defiance, Gloucester, Massachusetts
- Fort Dumpling, Newport, Rhode Island
- Fort George a.k.a. Fort St. Michael, Pensacola, Florida
- Fort George, Castine, Maine
- Fort Independence, Boston, Massachusetts
- Fort Johnson, Charleston, South Carolina
- Fort Johnston, Wilmington, North Carolina
- Fort Marion a.k.a. Beaufort Battery, Port Royal, South Carolina
- Fort McClary, Portsmouth, Maine
- Fort Mifflin, Philadelphia, Pennsylvania
- Fort Miller, Marblehead, Massachusetts
- Fort Monroe, Chesapeake Bay, Virginia
- Fort Nathan Hale, New Haven, Connecticut
- Fort Pickering, Salem, Massachusetts
- Fort Pownall, Penobscot, Maine
- Fort Sewall, Marblehead, Massachusetts
- Fort Stanwyx, Rome, New York
- Fort Wadsworth a.k.a Fort Tompkins, Staten Island, New York
- Fort Wolcott, Newport, Rhode Island
- Old Fort Niagara, Youngstown, New York

After the colonial period and prior to the first American system of forts, the Revolutionary War saw increased use of preexisting French and British forts. Many of these installations were tailored to specific American needs but due to a lack of a comprehensive plan, they proved to be a bonanza. Some of the forts had been used during the colonial period and thus saw further service. Geographical clusters indicate areas of importance. Here is a brief list of some but not all the forts that played an important part in the Revolutionary War. Some are still in existence in one form or the other; many are not and have been lost forever.

Critical Revolutionary War Forts

- Battery Conanicut, Jamestown, Rhode Island
- Fort Acushnet, New Bedford, Massachusetts
- Fort Allen, Portland, Maine
- Fort Black Rock, Fairfield, Connecticut
- Fort Dumpling, Jamestown, Rhode Island
- Fort George, Castine, Maine
- Fort Griswold, New London, Connecticut
- Fort Independence, Boston, Massachusetts
- Fort Johnson, Wilmington, North Carolina
- Fort Knyphausen, New York City, New York
- Fort Lee, Ft. Lee, New Jersey
- Fort Liberty, Newport, Rhode Island
- Fort McHenry, Baltimore, Maryland
- Fort Mercer, Red Bank, New Jersey
- Fort Mifflin, Philadelphia, Pennsylvania
- Fort Miller, Marblehead, Massachusetts
- Fort Nathan Hale, New Haven, Connecticut
- Fort Nelson, Norfolk, Virginia
- Fort O'Brian, Machiasport, Maine
- Fort Phoenix, New Bedford, Massachusetts
- Fort Pownall, Penobscot, Maine
- Fort Revere, Boston, Massachusetts
- Fort Richmond, Staten Island, New York
- Fort Saybrook, Old Saybrook, Connecticut

- Fort Sewall, Marblehead, Massachusetts
- Fort Stark, Portsmouth, New Hampshire
- Fort Sullivan, Portsmouth, Maine
- Fort Washington, Portsmouth, New Hampshire
- Long Point Fort, Stonington, Connecticut

Necessity is the mother of invention, and times of war invariably and inevitably bring out the best and worst in men. The iconic forts designed by Simon Bernard had their genesis hundreds of years ago primarily in his native France. Between these nascent beginnings there were several iterations and elaborate plans on how to efficiently protect Florida's (and America's) long, eastern coastline from naval bombardment and blunt or deter possible invasion by a foreign power.

The Treaty of Amity and Commerce signed in France in 1776 by Benjamin Franklin formally stated that France recognized the United States as an independent nation. The Treaty of Alliance made the United States and France allies against Great Britain, thus paving the way for some of France's most brilliant military minds to give much-needed advice to the newly established nation. There were other Frenchmen who preceded Bernard who laid the groundwork for his eventual rise to prominence.

Sébastien Le Prestre de Vauban was born in a small village in Burgundy, France, in 1633 into a provincially noble family that had a few connections. In his early military career he served Louis de Bourbon, who was also known as the Prince of Condé. The rash, pretentious, but nevertheless tactically sound Condé led a revolt against his cousin the young King Louis XIV in what was a civil war. Although Vauban was captured by royalists, he impressed the king's Italian adviser, Cardinal Jules Mazarin and was given the opportunity to switch sides after the royalists won the civil war.

France was in the process of conquering the Spanish Nether-lands (present-day Belgium and Luxembourg) and, within short order, parts of Artois, Picardy, and Flanders were controlled by the French. As luck for Vauban would have it, the king's chief engineer, Louis Nicolas de Clerville, was sick, enabling the king to give Vauban the opportunity to prove his mettle.

His reputation as an engineer grew during the war with Spain, when he began to develop his theories. During the reign of Louis XIV, he not only developed a close relationship with the king but also with the Marquis de Louvois, who was the king's secretary of war. Vauban's proposals, which emphasized fighting wars sophisticatedly and with a minimum loss of men, greatly appealed to the king.

At the time, all forts were star forts characterized by arith-metical designs to be overlaid on each other. In doing so these forts could resist the effects of cannon fire. The high walls of medieval castles had been replaced by steeply sloped embank-ments that were resistant to the often-disastrous results of being bombarded by cannonballs. The forts that Vauban designed had straight-sided moats, and the walls were constructed from indigenous resources.

Cannon were placed high on the ramparts while small open-ings in the walls allowed for crude but effective small-arms fire usually in the form of a harquebus. Natural, obviously defen-sive features such as hills and rivers were cleverly incorporated into the designs. The Italians had also integrated these types of forts into their defenses and years later they were not unknown in the United States.

Vauban also adopted what was known as a *pre carre*, which roughly translates as a dueling field, square field, or fence of iron that leveled out a border and was in turn supported by two or three lines of impenetrable, interrelated fortresses that acted in concert with one another and had a symbiotic relationship for their mutual benefit. The reasoning was that the garrisons in these fortresses would be strong enough to delay an invading force until reinforcements arrived. The Spanish Netherlands was reinforced with a fence of iron whose efficacy would last until World War I. France's northern border was similarly fortified between 1668 and 1698.

This was a period of almost continuous warfare beginning in 1672 when King Louis XIV assaulted the Dutch Republic. Subsequently England, Spain, Austria, the Netherlands, and the German princely states were scenes of battles and fortresses that were bombarded, besieged, and stormed. The carnage ended in 1697 at the end of the Nine Years' War, also known as the War of the League of Augsburg.

By the time his career ended, Vauban was credited as having built 33 forts and fortified walled towns and made stronger about 300 others. The designs of Fort Ticonderoga and Fort William Henry in New York and Fort Monroe in Virginia are some of the examples of the influence he had on fort design.

He also designed the socket bayonet that attached to the outside of a soldier's firearm, rather than inside the muzzle as the previously used plug bayonet had done, and the innovative tactic of ricochet gunfire. He favored the French army using the new flintlock musket that would replace the less-efficient matchlock musket.

Together these two adaptions influenced the decline of what was called the age of the Spanish tercio that armed massed infantry with a combination of muskets and pikes. In turn, these allowed commanders to organize their infantrymen in thinner formations, revolutionizing tactics. Vauban also built permanent barracks for French soldiers and created the first professionally proficient force of military engineers.

But his greatest contribution, one that eventually was adopted by American military leaders, was to build a series of forts that ringed the roughly square shape of France. At the time France had approximately 2,595 miles of international borders. Although there was peace for the time being there was no guarantee it would last.

The 12 forts that Vauban built from north to south in a clockwise direction and are UNESCO World Heritage Sites are: Arras, Longwy, Neuf-Brisach, Besancon, Briancon, Mont-Dauphin, Ville Franche-de-ConBent, Mont-Louis, Blaye/Cussac-Fort Medoc, Saint-Martin-de-Re, and finally on the Brittany coast Camaret-sur-Mer, and Saint-Vaast-la-Hougue.

By doing so Vauban secured and stabilized France's new borders. It was elegant in its simplicity and possessed a logic worthy of Aristotle. The Americans would make several attempts to replicate what Vauban had accomplished and, in the end, it would be another Frenchman who would make Florida's borders secure.

American military commanders had knowledge of Vauban's techniques specifically as it applied to siege warfare. His system involved digging a trench three to four feet deep parallel to the protective guns of a city or fort but beyond the range of the city's or fort's cannons or rifle fire. The dirt used to create the trench was used to create a parapet.

Then the attackers dug a second trench diagonally toward the city or fort in a zigzag fashion until the attacker's artillery could reach the city or fort. A second parallel trench was dug, artillery was moved into this trench and the assault was begun.

On September 28, 1781, 16,000 American and French soldiers led by General George Washington and the French commander Comte de Rochambeau lay siege to the Virginia town of Yorktown, which was held by British General Charles Cornwallis. Utilizing Vauban's technique, it took the Americans and French about three weeks before the British finally surrendered.

The defeat at Yorktown ended for all intents and purposes major conflicts in North America. Claiming to be sick, General Cornwallis sent Brigadier General Charles O'Hara in his place while General Washington sent his second-in-command Benjamin Lincoln to formally accept Cornwallis's sword.

With the advent of Napoleon's stupendous victories in Europe that emphasized mass frontal assaults, Vauban whose theories had reached their zenith, was replaced by the French-Swiss officer Antoine-Henri Jomini. Now the prominence was on offensive strategies. Jomini's teachings were the principal theories that ruled how war was fought. His ideas were customary reading at many military academies, including the United States Military Academy at West Point, New York. His adherents included many officers who served in the Civil War. Jomini was eventually succeeded by Carl Philipp Gottfried von Clausewitz, a Prussian general and theorist after the 1870 Franco-Prussian War. Jomini also served in the Russian army.

Jomini's theories did not go unnoticed in the United States. After graduating first in the class of 1824 at West Point, Army engineer Dennis Hart Mahan went to Europe, where he studied at the highly respected School of Engineering and Artillery in Metz, France. After returning to the United States in 1830, he accepted a teaching job at West Point.

Mahan disagreed with Jomini's precepts that stressed offense over defense because he realized that American armies were led by professional, well-trained officers who commanded nonprofessional, everyday citizenry in militias. He rejected the idea of wasting the lives of these well-intended men in mass frontal assaults where large numbers of casualties in the form of killed or wounded were almost guaranteed. Instead, he favored heavily fortified earthworks or field fortifications, as did Vauban. Mahan reasoned that these strong defensive positions would force an attacker to launch futile frontal assaults. The failure of these assaults with their attendant mass casualties would result in a loss of morale and a will to fight and ensure victory for the defenders,

Jomini had also rejected this idea, reasoning that outmaneuvering an adversary with a huge army was difficult if not impossible. Napoleon's numerous successes was solely due to his innate tactical genius that would be impossible to duplicate.

As was the case with Vauban, technological advances dramatically altered conventional military strategy. In 1846 the French army officer Claude-Etienne Minie invented the Minie ball and three years later the Minie rifle that had a rifled groove on the inside of its barrel. This caused the Minie ball or Minie bullet to spin and increased its accuracy. In addition, combined with the Minie, rifle range was also increased substantially. Minie was later a manager at the Remington Arms Company in the United States and he also served as an instructor for the Khedive of Egypt.

Smoothbore rifles had an effective range of between 100 and 160 yards. The Minie rifle's range was up to 500 yards, more than twice the distance. In a practical sense, if the defenders of a fort were armed with Minie rifles they could kill or wound attackers at a greater distance than defenders armed with smoothbore rifles. Because they were out of range of the smoothbore rifles, the defenders were also safer and could fire their weapons with relative impunity.

Mass assaults thus became extremely perilous. This was painfully evident during the first battles of the Civil War although prior military theorists did not recognize the immediate impact the new rifles would have.

As a result, Mahan preached building forts with not only earthworks for maximum protection, but he also incorporated Vauban's system of trenches into the defenses. The only way an attacking force could hope to succeed would be to launch a frontal assault that would invariably fail while at the same time taking mass casualties.

Although Mahan taught his theories to his students at West Point, where the top 10 to 20 percent of graduates became military engineers, many were still influenced by Jomini. Both viewpoints were utilized during the Civil War, after which generals on both sides realized the futility of frontal assaults using huge numbers of men.

The sometimes prescient, usually cigar-smoking Lieutenant General Ulysses S. Grant realized this and adhered to Vauban's and by extension Mahan's instructions when he wisely opted not to initiate a frontal assault on Petersburg, Virginia, but chose siege tactics instead of frontal attacks on the Confederate earthwork forts.

Although Grant's Union army had between 67,000 and 125,000 men versus the Confederate's 52,000, he would be constructing more than 30 miles of trenches that ran from Richmond's eastern fringes to the eastern and southern peripheries of Petersburg. The siege, a series of bitterly fought separate battles, began on June 15, 1865, and ended on April 2, 1865, with a Union victory. Mahan's concepts were justified, and Grant triumphed.

The Union trenches averaged six to eight feet wide and were about three feet deep. The excavated earth was used to create parapets. The walls of the trenches were prevented from collapsing by bolstering them with either rough logs or sandbags. Running along the bottom of the trench was a fire step, a shelf that soldiers could stand on and fire at the enemy over the parapet. Two-man rifle pits used as sentry posts were spaced out evenly in front of the first line of trenches.

In addition to these trenches that stayed true to the zigzag configurations prescribed by Vauban, long, straight trenches connected the rear elements of the army with the frontline troops. These trenches were quite deep and covered with wood planks or logs, so they were for the most part out of sight of the enemy. In some instances, the trenches were deep enough so that wagons could travel along them well below ground level.

Both sides provided protection for their men from artillery bombardment in the form of small, claustrophobia-inducing shelters dug into the sides of the trenches or separate, small huts made of timber where small groups of men could huddle in almost complete darkness. Reminiscent of the spikes that protected Julius Caesar's fortified camps that he established when he conquered Gaul, requisitioned fence rails were stuck in the earth facing the enemy and both sides also employed sharpened tree limbs or the tops of trees whose branches had been sharpened for the same purpose. The trenches and impediments to attacks were to a great extent a precursor and almost exact analogues to the infamous World War I trenches in both their form and functionality. Many Union artillerymen opportunistically requisitioned furnishings such as small couches and tables from proximate homes to make life a little more comfortable in the trenches.

While Mahan basked in satisfaction as the Confederate stronghold was slowly and methodically subdued, another more ambitious plan was being proposed, a plan that in concept but not quite execution was approaching Simon Bernard's ultimate solution.

An anaconda is defined as an exceptionally long, heavy South American snake of the boa family or any similar large snake that crushes its victims to death in its coils.

The first comprehensive plan to end the revolt of southern states was put forth by General Winfield Scott to President Abraham Lincoln in which all Confederate ports were to be blockaded while an army of up to 80,000 men would split the

Confederacy in two by taking control of the Mississippi River. It was called the Anaconda Plan.

Born near Petersburg, Virginia, on June 13, 1786, Scott had already established himself as a more-than-competent leader beginning in the War of 1812 where he fought in the battle of Queenstown Heights and the battle of Fort George. His exploits continued in the battle of Chippawa or the battle of Lundy's Lane, where he received significant injuries that took him six months to recover from.

The muttonchop-wearing Scott was a participant in the Niagara crisis that involved the capturing of Montreal, taking control of the St. Lawrence River and cutting off upper Canada from lower Canada, the Nullification Crisis, and the Black Hawk War during the 1830s, during which he was instrumental in putting an end to the war. He also took part in the Second Seminole War and the Creek War in 1836.

Five years later he was the commanding general of the United States army and when the Mexican-American War erupted in 1846, he subsequently captured the port city of Veracruz. At the battle of Cerro Gordo, the battle of Contreras, and the battle of Churubusco, his opponent was none other than General Antonio López de Santa Anna, who conquered the Alamo between February 23 and March 6, 1836. Scott also captured Mexico City.

The Mississippi was (and still is) the equivalent of a modern-day interstate highway. Corn, meat, lumber, wheat, and other goods came from the Midwest while valuable tobacco and cotton found their way to New Orleans. Needed and wanted European materials flowed upriver.

The tactically sound Scott had carefully outlined his plan. Heavily armed gunboats would secure the river from Cairo, Illinois, all the way south to the Gulf of Mexico. Amphibious strike forces supported by the gunboats would also be utilized to seize rebel positions along the way while the larger force would follow and engage in more conventional warfare. Scott believed that rebel-held forts and other strongholds would fall sequentially like dominoes. The regular army would follow and protect and secure the victories.

The penultimate battles would entail the taking of the Confederate forts situated below New Orleans. Once this was accomplished, the Mississippi River would be completely under Union control, and the uprising would effectively be cut in half. The west would be separated and isolated from the south. Once this was accomplished and the rebels no longer had access to their resources the only course of action remaining would be to surrender.

The irreversible division of the Confederacy into two separate, indefensible entities would occur when the Tennessee River Valley was conquered followed by subjugating Georgia to Union control. The capitulation of Richmond, Virginia, capital of the Confederate States of America, would surely follow. When the South was finally sealed off, Union partisans would exert political pressure on Confederate governors and force them to capitulate.

Scott's protégé, Major General George B. McClellan, who was born in Philadelphia on December 3, 1826, of Scots-Irish heritage, was not very sanguine when Scott told him about his plan. The son of a well-known surgeon, it was noted by McClellan, whose son George B. McClellan Jr. would later serve as the mayor of New York city from 1904 to 1909, that the Anaconda Plan failed to state how many men and support troops would be needed to effectively guard a minimum of 3,000 to perhaps as many as 3,500 miles of coastline controlled by the rebellious states. Distribution of available assets wasn't mentioned either nor was there a time line.

Because he felt there was little synergy between the different elements of the plan, McClellan made a counterproposal that involved 80,000 men who would attack Virginia via the Kenawha Valley and head directly toward Richmond. The second part of the proposal had the same 80,000 men marching south where they would cross the Ohio River and invade Kentucky and Tennessee.

Furthermore, all the gunships would have to be steam powered and because of the relatively short period of time they could be operational before having to replenish their fuel supply, it was imperative that the Union be in control of a suitable harbor near the southern terminus of the blockade that could function as a refueling station. In the absence of such a harbor the gunships would spend an extraordinary amount of time returning to their home port to take on more fuel.

At the time, the Union Navy consisted of a paltry 90 ships. To make matters worse, only 42 were steam powered and therefore fit for blockade duty, hardly enough to patrol not only the coastlines but also at least by conservative estimates 12 main ports, some of which, like New Orleans and Mobile, were quite large. New crews would obviously have to be trained, and that would take time, and some of the ships would need repairs before they could become fully operational.

Commercial ships were hastily retrofitted and shipbuilding increased so that by the end of the war the number increased to 671. It was also acknowledged that at least one major port yet to be determined would have to be taken by force, implying an occupation of a large Confederate possession that would obviously be preceded by a fight whose duration was not yet known.

Moreover, on April 19, 1861, President Lincoln ordered in his Proclamation of Blockade Against Southern Ports that all the ports of the rebelling states from Carolina to Texas be blockaded. When Virginia and North Carolina seceded, their shorelines were added as well. Lincoln's proclamation, in effect until the end of the war, subsumed Scott's Anaconda Plan.

Superimposed on top of not only the Anaconda Plan but also Lincoln's proclamation was the Blockade Strategy Board, also known as the Commission of Conference or the DuPont Board, which was convened in the summer of 1861 at the behest of the Navy Department and with delegates from the Army and the Treasury Department. The purpose of the Board was to determine how the blockade was to be maintained.

At the time, hydrographic information on the Atlantic coast was fairly accurate, but completely lacking on the Gulf of Mexico. In the absence of such knowledge, the Board stated and strongly suggested that a Coast Survey ship was to be integrated into each blocking squadron. Additionally, the Board considered what types of ships were going to be used by both sides, the values of the numerous southern ports, and the force the blockading ships were likely to be met with.

The Board made several other recommendations as well. At least one section of the South Carolina coast would have to be occupied. The choices were Bull's Head Bay, St. Helena Sound, and Port Royal Sound. Port Royal was in Union hands in late 1861 and used to almost completely blockade Savannah. Fernandina, Florida, was to be taken and used as the southern terminus of the Atlantic coast blockading line. This was accomplished on March 1, 1862.

The Confederates changed their strategy after they were beaten at Fort Henry and Fort Donelson, both in Tennessee and Roanoke Island in North Carolina. The rebel armies would now be focused on the critical interior. As a result, thousands of men and their equipment were removed from the coast, leaving only the major ports of Savannah, Wilmington, and Charleston on the Atlantic coast to be defended. For the duration of the war, only eight steam-powered blockade-running ships would sneak into Georgia or north Florida ports. As it pertained to the Gulf of Mexico, the Confederacy adapted its strategic planning as well leaving only Mobile (Alabama), New Orleans (Louisiana) and Galveston (Texas) protected.

In the end, the efficacy of the blockade was questioned. Nimble blockade runners evaded capture three quarters of the time. Small and built for speed, the runners easily outran the larger, heavier ships trying to stop or intercept them. Size and speed sacrificed carrying capacity, but that in and of itself did not hamper the Confederates from supplying their armies with badly needed supplies.

Owners and crews of standard freight-carrying ships that could carry larger loads than the blockade runners took their business elsewhere, crippling the Confederate economy. The rebels' main export, cotton, could not reach its intended markets in Europe, and that in turn greatly crimped the Confederate economy.

The Blockade Strategy Board had a trifling influence on the war, but it was a portent of organizational hierarchy, namely a staff system. The Anaconda Plan was never formally adopted but it did have a reincarnation of sorts in the form of a dual land thrust in 1864 that saw Lieutenant General Ulysses S. Grant plow his way through Virginia and Tennessee while Major General William T. Sherman steamrolled through Georgia all the way to the Atlantic Ocean.

Prior to the Civil War, the groundwork and foundation had already been laid for a system whose uniformity would within a relatively short period of time ensure America's sovereignty and protect it against the armed incursions that typically came from naval bombardment.

The first American system of coastal fortifications circa 1794 to 1808 was characterized by somewhat crude, easy-to-construct open forts with earth parapets. A system of bastions where the walls were laid out at angles made the forts resemble stars. Anywhere from 10 to a couple of dozen guns, a miscellaneous assortment of iron and brass cannons American, British or French from the Revolutionary War, were positioned on the parapets.

The largest guns were 24-pounders, but many were smaller. While some of the cannons were mounted on carriages that could traverse from side to side and follow a moving ship at sea, many cannons were on non-traversing carriages that prohibited them from tracking from side to side, obviously an impediment when trying to disable an attacking ship. The use of traversing carriages was adopted from the more-advanced French artillery system.

Although it was mandated by the federal government, the money for the forts was supplied by individual states, whose governors had the final approval of how the funds were to be allocated. Governors in turn delegated responsibility to political appointees who in many cases had their own interests at heart. As a result, there was little consistency in the design of First System forts. Existing forts were upgraded in many cases and new ones were built, resulting in an assortment that reflected no clear-cut, singular vision.

Forts previously built by the French and British were occupied and used by the Americans during the Revolutionary War. While adequate, they were by no means a long-term solution for protecting an entire nation. The United States Corps of Engineers was founded in 1802 and established a school at West Point. President Thomas Jefferson wisely made coastal fortification a priority. The First System was made official by an act of Congress on March 20, 1794.

The problem was that America had no engineers who would design and oversee the design and construction of 21 harbor forts. Fortunately, there was a glut of out-of-work

French engineers, some of whom had served with the Continental Army during the Revolutionary War. Thus, the influx of French-born engineers began.

After the French Royal Corps of Engineers rejected Stephen Rochefontaine, who was born Étienne Nicolas Marie Béchet, Sieur de Rochefontaine in Ay, Marne, France, Rochefontaine crossed the Atlantic and arrived in America in 1778. He volunteered his services to General Washington's Continental Army and was given the rank of Captain in the Corps of Engineers. He served with distinction during the siege of Yorktown. After a brief stay, he returned to France, where he functioned as an infantry officer before coming back to America. In 1794, as a civilian engineer, he was tasked with fortifying the entire New England coast.

Another enterprising Frenchman seeking employment was Louis de Tousard, who soldiered with Marie-Joseph Paul Yves Roch Gilbert du Motier, Marquis de Lafayette, who was known simply as Lafayette, who came to America to seek fame and fortune after being commissioned in France at the tender age of 13. Lafayette served with distinction, allowing Tousard to use his association with him to become an Inspector of Artillery by 1800. Lafayette also led American soldiers at the siege of Yorktown.

Although Tousard's greatest contribution was the notion of interchangeable parts for guns, Tousard, who was an artillerist by trade, did design Fort Adams and also contributed to the design of Fort Hamilton in Newport, Rhode Island. He also contributed to the founding of the United States Military Academy.

Pierre Charles L'Enfant was with General Washington at Valley Forge, serving on his general staff. An artist by trade he was commissioned by Lafayette to paint a portrait of Washington. Although L'Infant never designed any fortifications, he did make an important contribution when he designed the basic plan for Washington, D.C.

A Frenchman who did design American forts was Jean-François Foncin, a graduate of the École royale du génie de Mézières who arrived in America in January 1797. He designed the iconic Fort McHenry in Baltimore, Maryland, among others.

Most First System forts were relatively small and only had one casement or tier on which cannon were mounted. Sometimes water batteries or cannon emplacements, were added in front of the forts when feasible to offer more protection. Often, they were garrisoned by only several hundred men and sometimes fewer than that. But as a whole they were far better than those that came before them because they were stronger defensively and offensively.

Several of the forts were rehabilitations of colonial forts, which was a relatively quick upgrade that required less labor, time, and money. They were Fort Constitution in Portsmouth, New Hampshire, Fort Independence in Boston, Massachusetts, Fort Wolcott in Newport, Rhode Island, and Fort Mifflin in Philadelphia, Pennsylvania. The vulnerable East Coast was incrementally being strengthened and was a harbinger of what was to come in the near future.

FLORIDA DISCOVERED

*O*n March 4, 1513, three ships and about 200 men set sail from Puerto Rico. They crossed open water for almost a month until April 2, 1513, when what was believed to be another island was sighted. Because the supposed island had a lush countryside and because it was the Easter season the Spaniards called Pascua Florida or Festival of Flowers, de León named it La Florida.

The following day they came ashore, probably near St. Augustine, although on the east coast other historians believe it may have been farther south near the present location of Melbourne Beach. Two days later, the mini armada reached and named Biscayne Bay and replenished their dwindling water supplies at Key Biscayne, which was originally known as Santa Maria.

Heading south, de León sailed parallel to the Florida Keys trying to find a gap so he and his men could head north and explore the west coast. On May 23, succeeding in reaching the west coast they were met by the native Calusa Indians, who drove them off with fusillades of arrows launched from sea canoes. Licking their wounds, the tiny expedition doggedly chugged north eventually making landfall in the vicinity of Charlotte Harbor, although some experts are of the opinion it was either Tampa Bay or even Pensacola where they dropped anchor.

While taking on water and making much-needed repairs to their three battered ships, de León and his men were again attacked by the Calusa near what is now Sanibel Island. There were casualties on both sides, and the Spaniards took eight Calusa captives who described a chain of islands that lay to the west.

The bulldog-tenacious de León reached the tiny islands barely above sevel level that comprise the Dry Tortugas on June 12, where they hunted turtles, Caribbean monk seals, and seabirds to supplement their diet. Guided by their intrepid chief pilot Anton de Alaminos, they then headed southwest to circle around Cuba so they could return home to Puerto Rico. On July 9, the three ships reached the Grand Bahamas, and the fleet was disbanded. After eight months, Ponce de León safely returned to Puerto Rico, and from there he made his way to Spain, where he was knighted and given a personal coat of arms.

Several unauthorized voyages by men looking to usurp his claim on Florida prompted a last, fateful, colonizing voyage led by de León. An expedition of 200 men that included farmers, priests, and artisans plus 50 horses and agricultural implements landed on Florida's southwest coast near Charlotte Harbor or the Caloosahatchee River, an area with which DeLeon was familiar.

Meeting stiff resistance from the indigenous Calusa Indians, de León was wounded by a poisoned arrow. The attempt at colonizing Florida was abandoned, and the expedition returned to Havana, Cuba, where de León succumbed to his wound. He was later buried in Puerto Rico.

Over half a century later, in 1565, another Spanish admiral and explorer, Pedro Menéndez de Avilés, set sail to Florida to find his son Juan who had been shipwrecked there in 1561. Avilés had gained his reputation by commanding the treasure fleets from Mexico and the Caribbean back to Spain. When the French established an outpost in Jacksonville named Fort Caroline, Avilés was ordered to destroy it and settle the region.

Toward that end, on August 28, 1565, Aviles landed in Florida and established San Agustín or Saint Augustine. The site was chosen because it not only had an abundant supply of fresh water from an artesian spring but also was very defensible.

After slaughtering survivors from three storm-wrecked ships who had sailed to attack Saint Augustine, Aviles constructed a huge fort in Saint Augustine used as a base for gold and silver-laden ships being sent to Spain and a smaller fort not far away near an inlet. The Spanish had gained a toehold in what was to become the United States, but would they be able to consolidate their gains?

Nothing stays the same especially where worldwide domination is the object.

Despite the heroic exploration and conquest carried out by the conquistadores, who were in many instances educated, well-connected Cortés and Pizarro being exceptions, sophisticated men of noble birth who braved incredible hardships far from home and sent galleons of treasure back to Spain, it was not quite enough. Spain had ports in Veracruz, Acapulco, Havana, Cartagena de Indies, Lima, and half a world away in Manila, the largest city in the vast archipelago that comprised the Philippines and that was critical for trade with China. Goods from Asia crossed the vast expanses of the Pacific Ocean to Acapulco, Mexico, and from there were shipped back to Spain.

The number of immigrants eventually rose so high that it was impossible for the Spanish to supply them with much-needed goods. Moreover, Spain's army and navy were stretched almost to the breaking point across Europe and the Mediterranean. Improved French and Dutch armed forces were a viable threat to Spanish supremacy.

Slowly but surely, France became dominant in Europe, while the English, Dutch, and French established permanent colonies in the Caribbean. The English chose sugar-rich St. Kitts, Nevis,

Barbados, Antigua, Jamaica, and Monserrat, while the French settled in Guadeloupe and Martinique, and the Dutch opted for St. Martin, Curacao, and St. Eustace.

These colonies provided an enormous amount of wealth to the English and Dutch. Spain simply could not afford to pay for the consumer goods. Most of the goods were manufactured by Europeans. Costs associated with the defense of the empire also rose. Although gold and silver were still being transported to Spain, it was not enough. Spain was slowly being bled to death economically. Spain's expenses were greater than its income and the eventual result was never in doubt. Spain was the greatest maritime power the world had ever seen. It dominated Portugal, Sicily, Naples, and the Rhineland in Germany. Its power extended from current-day Canada south to Patagonia, and it controlled lucrative trading posts in India and Southeast Asia as well as holdings in New Guinea and North Africa. Spain was now hemorrhaging money.

Realizing the vulnerability of Spain, the opportunistic English made their move. Against a turbulent, multiyear background of local and global wars followed by intricate, almost byzantine treaties predicated by burgeoning and waning national interests, the English consolidated their hold on North America.

Jamestown on the Chesapeake Bay, later to become Virginia, was the first prosperous colony established in 1607, followed 13 years later by a second permanent colony in Plymouth. Ten years later, a third colony, the Massachusetts Bay Colony, was founded.

In 1670 the English captured Tortola from the Dutch and soon annexed Anegada and Virgin Gorda, nearby islands. These would later become the British Virgin Islands. Previously uninhabited Barbados had been settled years earlier.

Methodically and incrementally, the British founded more colonies: The Province of Maryland and the Province of

Carolina later to be divided into North Carolina and South Carolina, the Province of Pennsylvania, the Province of New Jersey, the Province of New York (formerly Dutch-named New Amsterdam), and the Province of Delaware.

Although the French had solidified their grip on Quebec City on the St. Lawrence River, the epicenter of the French colony in Canada, they lost the territories of Newfoundland and Acadia. The latter was to be named Nova Scotia.

Either presciently or seeing an opportunity to stem the increasing and stifling British influence and possibly recover territories lost to Britain, particularly Florida, and to maintain its hold on Spanish Louisiana, Spain, in a last-ditch effort to salvage years of colonization in North America, formed an alliance with France. Huge tracts of lands were rapidly changing hands. France surrendered territories east of the Mississippi River to Britain while at the same time ceding lands west of the Mississippi to Spain, which gave Florida to the British, who created the provinces not only of East Florida and West Florida but also of Quebec.

Out of necessity and hopeful empiricism, and angry at having lost much territory, Spain and France became unlikely bedfellows. Through the port of New Orleans, from warehouses in Havana and from the northwestern Spanish port of Gardoqui, Spain aided the nascent revolution materially in the form of arms and financially. Because they were ideologically and philosophically sympathetic to the American Revolution, viewing it as a replication of the basic tenets and ideals espoused by the French Revolution, specifically the embodiment of the enlightenment life-force against British oppressiveness, France readily supplied gunpowder, cannons, clothing, and shoes that were funneled to the revolutionaries.

An estimated 12,000 soldiers and 32,000 sailors were also sent to America during the revolution. Aid passed through the neutral Dutch West Indies port of Saint Eustatius. American ships were given haven in French ports. France also provided technical support, lending military strategists namely the Marquis de (Jean) Lafayette.

Fought between 1756 and 1763, the Seven Years' War was a global slugfest that affected the Philippines, India, West Africa, Europe, and the Americas. England, Prussia, Portugal, and the Electorate of Brunswick-Lüneburg squared off against France, Spain, Sweden, the Holy Roman Empire, and Russia. The war left hundreds of thousands, dead, wounded, or unfit for service. The sparks that ignited what was to become a global conflict were attacks on disputed French positions in North America by the British.

The Treaty of Paris, signed by Spain, France, and Britain and the Treaty of Hubertusburg between Austria, Prussia, and Saxony in 1763 ended the conflict. The results had enormous repercussions that reverberated throughout the world and the Americas.

Britain got the majority of New France in North America, Spanish Florida, some islands in the West Indies (specifically Guadeloupe and Martinique), the colony of Senegal in West Africa, and control of French trading posts on the Indian subcontinent. Spain lost Florida but got French Louisiana and regained control of its colonies in Cuba and the Philippines that had been captured by the British during the war. One of the tangential results was the British assault on Acadian populations in what is now Prince Edward Island, the St. John River valley, and the Petitcodiac River valley in 1755, a year prior to the official start of the hostilities that resulted in the expulsions of the Acadians to make room for English settlers.

A year before hostilities formally ended, France made a half-hearted attack on St. Johns, Newfoundland but was repulsed. The British were now firmly in control of all eastern

North America. Commingled with the global conflict was a smaller version that set as rivals the two-million-strong British inhabitants of British America versus the approximately 60,000 French settlers. The French enlisted the help of several native Indian tribes, notably the Ottawa, Lenape, Algonquin, and Ojibwa. The Catawba, Iroquois Confederacy, and several others threw in their lot with the British. The war inspired James Fenimore Cooper to write his iconic novel *The Last of the Mohicans.*

By all accounts this clash was characterized by guerrilla warfare and rampant atrocities committed by both sides. Added to the cost of the Seven Years' War, Britain's national debt was almost doubled. New taxes were imposed, and they were met with stiff resistance. When soldiers were sent to enforce British authority and reinforce England's rule, the colonies revolted. Two years after the revolution began and although the French had lost huge tracts of territory and seen their presence in the northern Caribbean dramatically reduced, they allied themselves with the Americans.

Although the Spanish were slowly but inexorably losing their grip on their valued possessions, they also allied themselves with the American rebels and once again crossed swords with the British. Aided by their newfound allies, the struggling rebels gradually gathered strength and self-confidence and eventually prevailed.

It took the newly created nation 18 years before it began its first attempts at building a series of both seacoast and riverine fortifications whose sole purpose was to protect the fledgling country from attack primarily from naval bombardment. Even though these forts were bastioned, meaning their corners jutted out so small cannon could provide covering fire to the outer walls, these early incarnations bore little resemblance to more complexly designed, existing forts found in Europe.

These initial fortifications were constructed of whatever materials were found either on-site or relatively near the site, enabling expeditious construction. Timber and earth were the primary resources along with brushwood. Many forts were simply open works with tall earth parapets on top of which an assortment of guns left over from the Revolutionary War could be brought to bear on attackers.

They were armed with whatever iron or brass cannons could be acquired regardless of caliber, age, or which country manufactured them. All the cannons worked the same way, and it made no practical difference if the guns were Spanish, British, or American. The only differences were that brass is softer than iron and that fact had to be taken into consideration in terms of rate of fire and size of projectile. Occasionally older guns would either misfire or in a worst-case scenario explode. Gun crew fatalities were common.

In addition to lending themselves to practical construction because the needed material was usually if not always abundantly available earthwork forts readily absorbed the impact and dispersed the energy caused by direct hits from cannonballs and obviously bullets. Damage created by the impact of heavy projectiles could easily be repaired simply by adding more earth. Knowing they were relatively safe increased the morale of the defenders and in turn exponentially reinforced discipline up the chain of command. Moreover, only a modicum of technical expertise in the construction of forts was required in the building of earthwork forts.

These forts are known collectively as the First American System. Their armament consisted primarily of 24-pounders and 42-pounders that refers to the weight of the spherical, solid shot i.e., a cannonball. A 42-pounder had a bore diameter of seven inches, a 32-pounder had a bore diameter of 6.4

inches, a 24-pounder had a bore diameter of 5.82 inches and an 18-pounder had a bore diameter of 5.3 inches.

The size of larger guns such as Columbiads that fired an 8-inch shell, mortars and howitzers that fired explosive-filled, hollow shells varied in weight because of the differences in the thicknesses of the shell walls. The caliber of these guns was expressed in inches. Rodman cannons developed later could fire 8-inch, 10-inch, 15-inch, and 20-inch shells for an impressive three miles.

Establishing a fort has since Roman times been called "castrametation." The first small cities to be fortified were scattered communities in the Indus Valley while in Mycenaean Greece large stone walls had been erected. A military garrison accommodated in a secure collection of buildings was known as a Greek "phrourion" and is comparable to an English fortress or castle.

The difference between a fort and a castle is that castles were the home of a monarch or nobleman. Castles flourished in Europe for centuries especially during the medieval period. They were obviously permanent, multistory structures unlike field fortifications such as earthwork structures that were not intended to last for extended periods of time.

The eleventh century saw the zenith of these strongholds that were huge buildings called motte and bailey castles. A motte is a mound forming the site of the castle and a bailey refers to housing for a king or a nobleman's lesser retinue. The king or nobleman and his retainers were housed in a keep. These structures were characterized by massively high, thick stone walls, moats, and a drawbridge. Although not replicated in America, they nevertheless exerted subtle influences in the minds of men who were to become instrumental in designing some of the iconic American fortresses.

In many instances, little remains of these forts except for pen-and-ink renderings, perhaps fading letters or buried in hard-to-find archival records obscure minutiae that to an extent reflected daily life. These forts were built with blood, sweat and tears as men often labored under the sweltering Florida sun, plagued by bloodsucking mosquitoes, drenching downpours, and violent lightning storms.

But it must not be forgotten that men lived in these forts, they cursed while doing grunt, backbreaking work under a scorching sun, they told ribald jokes, complained about the food, wrote letters to loved ones. For some, these installations were their final resting place.

FLORIDA'S LOST CATHEDRALS

*T*here are two recognized ways to measure the length of a coastline. The first method uses data from the U.S. Department of Commerce, National Oceanic and Atmospheric Administration and is based on lengths using large-scale nautical charts. This methodology excludes the Great Lakes coastlines. Only states with ocean coastline are included.

The second way to measure coastline lengths is from a list kept and maintained by the Office of Ocean and Resource Management of the National Oceanic and Atmospheric Administration. These lengths include tidal inlet areas that the first method does not include, but they do include Great Lakes coastlines that do not have similar tidal areas.

Using the first method Florida has 1,350 miles (2,170 kilometers) of coastline and using the second method 8,436 miles (13,576 kilometers). In contrast, using the first method Alaska has the longest coastline (6.640 miles or 10,690 kilometers) while New Hampshire has a paltry 13 miles (21 kilometers). Michigan, Wisconsin, Ohio, Minnesota, Pennsylvania, Illinois, Indiana, American Samoa, Guam, Northern Marianna Islands, Puerto Rico, and the US Virgin Islands are not included in the first method but are included in the second method. Obviously, these figures differ significantly due to the innate uncertainty at calculating coastlines.

Florida, a thumb-shaped peninsula, has an exceedingly long coastline that had to be protected. The correct placement of fortifications bearing in mind the current strategic objectives prevalent at the time and available ordinal assets (such as cannon) plus the anticipated strategic needs was of the utmost importance. To a large extent the future of America depended on the right decisions being made at the right time.

These forts that have not physically survived due to the ravages of time and neglect, but their memory continues untarnished.

FORT CAROLINE

Established: 1564
Location: St. Johns River, Jacksonville
Decommissioned: 1565

*T*o safeguard French claims to Florida, the Huguenot Jean Ribault and his men set foot on the site on the May River (now the St. Johns River) in February 1562 where they encountered Timucuan Indians prompting Ribault to move north to what is now South Carolina with 28 men and establish a settlement known as Charlesfort. The new settlement lasted one year. Ribault returned to Europe, where he was accused of being a spy and imprisoned by the English.

Not discouraged, Ribault's second-in-command, René Goulaine de Laudonnière, on a 1562 expedition, led 200 settlers back to Florida and brazenly established Fort Caroline on June 22, 1564. The site was a small open space created by the far western end of a high, steep bank that was later called St. Johns Bluff. The fort was intended to reinforce French claims in French Florida and give Huguenots a safe refuge from persecution.

Naturally, this attracted the attention of the Spanish, who were determined to maintain their hold in Florida. The French at the newly created fort who were planning to return to France were given a brief reprieve by an Englishman named John Hawkins who exchanged a small ship for four cannons, shot, powder and supplies. The French also gave Hawkins tobacco and he introduced it to England upon his return.

Fort Caroline, Jacksonville, Florida
FLORIDA MEMORY

The reprieve was short lived, however. In June 1565, Ribault got out of his English prison and promptly sailed back to Fort Caroline with a large fleet and hundreds of soldiers and settlers. Meanwhile the Spanish Governor of Florida, Don Pedro Menéndez de Avilés, had, at the same time been ordered to destroy the French outpost.

The French and Spanish fleets skirmished, the Spanish withdrew 35 miles to the south, founded St. Augustine, and when a ferocious storm delayed the pursuing Ribault an opportunistic Menéndez led his force overland during the storm and attacked Fort Caroline, the garrison of which had been reduced to between 200 and 250 people. The details of the resulting massacre can be seen in the chapter on Fort Matanzas. After obliterating Fort Caroline, the Spanish constructed their own fort named San Mateo on the same site but abandoned it in 1569. The precise location has never been determined.

Visitor Information

12713 Ft. Caroline Road, Jacksonville, FL 32225, (904) 641-7155, npsgov/timu, Call ahead for fees and hours.

Fort Caroline no longer exists. There is however an interpretive reconstruction of the fort that illustrates how the fort must have looked in the sixteenth century. What you see today is an informational model, a second iteration that is almost but not quite full scale.

The Fort Caroline National Memorial is on the National Register of Historic Places. Although it is a distinct National Park entity, the Memorial is managed as part of the Timucuan Ecological and Historical Preserve. Dolphins can be seen in the St. Johns River and there are well maintained nature trails and a visitor center that has a bookstore, an information desk, and an activity list. Additionally, there are three other areas well worth visiting.

Situated on top of St. Johns Bluff and having an unobstructed view of the St. Johns River, the marshes below, wildlife, and the Atlantic Ocean, the Ribault Monument memorializes Jean Ribault's landing in 1562.

The Theodore Roosevelt Area contains miles of hiking trails in a 600-acre combination of wetlands, hardwood forest and scrub vegetation.

Across from the entrance to Fort Caroline, National Memorial Spanish Pond was where Menéndez and his men camped. There is a boardwalk and trail that meanders through oak hammock, pine flatwoods, and a tidal marsh that abuts the Theodore Roosevelt Area. It is open from sunrise to sunset daily. Jacksonville is a bustling city that offers the intrepid visitor many opportunities in terms of cultural activities, sporting events, and fine dining.

FORT SAN MARCOS DE APALACHE

Established: 1718
Location: Wakulla Springs
Decommissioned: 1865

*S*mall, wooden outposts in the fecund territory of the Apalache Indians to produce wheat used to supply larger Spanish interests in the Caribbean had been previously built by the Spanish between 1697 and 1682 in the same area, on a peninsula at the confluence of the Wakulla River and the St. Marks River. Fire and wood rot possibly caused by limestone coating that, at least at a distance, made them look like they were made of stone, that doomed the previous iterations did not deter Captain Jose Primo de Ribera who started to build a wooden blockhouse in 1718 using wood harvested from the Mission San Luis de Apalache that lay to the north. The site is now the city of St. Marks.

The fort changed hands and names numerous times. The first fort built in 1679 was manned by 45 Spanish soldiers and 400 Apalache Indians. Three years later a coalition of Indian, French, and English attacked the Spanish colony whereupon the Spanish burned their fort and abandoned it.

When the Spanish returned in 1739, they started to build a larger, stronger stone fort, but before it could be completed West Florida was ceded to the British as part of the Treaty of Paris. To avoid confusion with the Castillo de San Marcos in St. Augustine, the British renamed the fort Fort St. Marks.

Fort San Marcos de Apalache, St. Marks, Florida
FLORIDA MEMORY

The British occupied the fort for the next 20 years as world powers jockeyed for favorable positions. Finally, France, Spain, Great Britain, and the newly founded United States through a series of treaties signed and agreed to in France in 1783, Britain gave Florida back to Spain and took possession in 1787 until 1818.

Despite its relatively small garrison, the fort played an integral part in the thriving Indian trade. However, that did not prevent it from being the target of local fights that involved British, French, Spanish, and American Indian cliques. A British traitor and former officer named William Augustus Bowles, who had formed a small, mixed-bag force of Europeans, American Indians, and Africans and led them against Spanish and British colonists, managed to wrest control of the lightly manned fort in the 1790s. The fort was retaken by a Spanish flotilla several weeks later.

About 30 years later, the fort's identity was finally settled in 1818 when Andrew Jackson invaded Florida during the First Seminole War. Soon after that the fort became American property when Spain ceded Florida to the United States in the Adams-Onis Treaty of 1819. General Jackson occupied the fort for almost a year and during that time a cemetery was created. In it 19 soldiers were buried. Dysentery and consumption were the main causes of death.

United States soldiers took control of the fort for three years while the government consolidated its hold on the new territory. It took 14 years after Florida became a state before United States Marines built a hospital at the fort to treat sufferers of an epidemic of yellow fever and sick sailors. Stones from the other fort were used. The hospital was completed in 1858.

For the next 100 years Fort San Marcos de Apalache a.k.a Fort St. Marks and Fort Ward, was owned privately and allowed to deteriorate. It was infested by undergrowth and accessible only by boat. Rehabilitation began in the 1960s when the site was bought by the state and declared a National Historic Landmark. The San Marcos de Apalache Historic State Park designation followed, and funds were allocated to fill in the marsh that separated it from the mainland, thus making it accessible to the general public.

Visitor Information

Fort San Marcos de Apalache, 148 Old Fort Road, St. Marks, FL 32355; (850) 925-6216; floridastateparks.org/parks-and-trails/san-marcos-de-apalache-historic-state-park

The park is 18 miles south of Tallahassee and was added to the National Register of Historic Places on November 13, 1966. Visitors are likely to see great blue herons, cormorants, gulls, anhingas, ospreys, pelicans, and other birds.

The museum houses artifacts such as pottery and tools. Programs and displays are on view at the top of the Marine hospital where visitors can see the original stone foundation. There is also an 18-minute video that encompasses the Spanish, English, Americans, and Confederates who occupied the site.

A favorite spot for fishing is Tucker's Point at the confluence of St. Marks River and the Wakulla River, where the two rivers flow into the Apalachee Bay. One of the things that makes it so attractive aside from the view is that fresh water and salt water come together. Anglers have caught sheepshead, speckled trout, redfish and occasionally Florida black bass. Be sure to check to see if a fishing license is required. Remember that all fish caught within the park must adhere to regulations relating to season, number, size, and method of capture.

There is ample parking and a long interpretive trail. The picnic area has tables and grills. Sea turtles, otters, squirrels, and, depending on the time of year and migratory patterns, manatees can be seen. Given two weeks' notice, a ranger-guided tour accommodating up to 50 people is available. Self-guided tour brochures can be found at the front gate entrance, inside the museum and near the cistern on the Wakulla River side of the museum.

Wakulla Springs is home to the world's largest and deepest freshwater springs, in which manatee sightings are common. For readers old enough to remember, the cult classic film *Creature from the Black Lagoon* was filmed here in 1954.

Although there is not a fort associated with this location, another place well worth visiting is the Natural Bridge Historic State Park.

NATURAL BRIDGE HISTORIC STATE PARK

*I*t was here that yet another change of hands occurred in 1861 when Confederates seized the fort and renamed it Fort Ward after Colonel George T. Ward, who owned Southwest Plantation, Waverly Plantation, and Clifford Plantation south of Tallahassee. New earthwork fortifications were erected and bolstered by a battery of cannon in order to defend the fort from a squadron of Union soldiers who had blockaded the St. Marks River throughout the war.

The battle of Natural Bridge was the last Confederate victory relative to the fort. It was fought in Woodville near Tallahassee on March 6, 1865. The Confederate forces consisted of the 1st Florida Militia, the 5th Florida Cavalry Battalion, the Kilcrease Artillery, Dunham's Battery, Abell's Battery, Company A of the Milton Light Artillery, Barwick's Company Reserves, Hodges' Company Reserves, Companies A, B, and F of the Florida Reserves, and reinforcements from Georgia, led by Brigade General William Miller and protected by breastworks. They prevented a joint force unit of United States Colored troops comprised of members from the 2nd Florida Cavalry, the 2nd U.S. Colored Infantry and the 99th U.S. Colored Infantry, led by Brigadier General John Newton, from crossing the quarter-mile-long Natural Bridge on the St. Marks River. Natural

Bridge is formed where the river drops into a sinkhole and flows underground for a quarter of a mile before emerging.

Confederate strength was approximately 1,000 men, including able-bodied troops, wounded troops, volunteers, and teenagers from the Florida Military and Collegiate Institute that would later become Florida State University. Union forces numbered approximately 700 troops. Union forces suffered 21 killed, 89 wounded, and 38 captured while the Confederates fared better with only three killed and 23 wounded.

Upon learning that Confederate forces had attacked both Cedar Keys and Fort Meyers and were supposed to be camped somewhere around Fort Ward, the Union General Newton advanced past the East River Bridge forcing the Confederate 5th Cavalry to withdraw to the Newport Bridge on the St. Marks River. A Union flotilla had arrived in Apalachee Bay between March 1 and March 3. Because Navy gunboats had previously run aground in the shallow waters of the St. Marks River, the flotilla approached cautiously.

Volunteers from Tallahassee, the only capital of the Confederacy not captured by Union forces during the Civil War, now had enough strength to force General Newton to circle around to Natural Bridge. On March 5, Brigadier General Miller ordered Confederate forces under the command of Lieutenant Colonel George Scott on an overnight march to defend Natural Bridge. The Confederates had made a countermove utilizing troops from their cavalry and volunteers.

The following day consisted of violent skirmishes along the narrow bridge that lasted for 10 hours. Gibson, still having trouble in the shallow waters, moved to engage the enemy, but his ships had trouble navigating the river and attempting to cross it at Natural Bridge. Confederate forces gave ground but still held the bridge.

On the evening of March 7, Union troops were under the protection of their fleet. Two sailors from the USS *Hendrick Hudson*, Seaman John Mack and Coxswain George Schutt, who had gone ashore to engage Confederate soldiers, were awarded the Congressional Medal of Honor for their heroic actions.

The *Hudson* was a 460-ton screw steamboat built at Greenpoint, New York in 1859 as the commercial steamship *Florida*. The Confederacy seized the ship in New Orleans in January 1962, and it saw extensive service as a blockade runner. On February 19, it carried cotton to Cuba and a month later returned to the Florida panhandle carrying rifles and gunpowder. On April 9, 1862, it was captured by the US *Bark* and subsequently renamed *Hendrick Hudson*. After capturing, ramming, and sinking Confederate blockade runners, it was decommissioned in August 1865 and sold. Then it returned to commercial service as a steamship and was wrecked near Havana on November 13, 1867.

Another Union attack on May 12, 1865, was more successful and Fort Ward fell to the Union.

Freshwater fishing on the north side of Natural Bridge is allowed and encouraged. Catfish, bream, crappie, Florida black bass, and if you're lucky, a striper can be caught. Remember that FWC fishing regulations pertaining to size, number, capture method, and season are enforced.

There are meandering hiking trails and picnic areas. A ranger-guided tour for groups up to 50 people (two weeks' notice, please) can be arranged. Call for fees and availability. A monument that honors Confederate soldiers who defended Natural Bridge is prominently displayed.

This site is unique because there is a reenactment of the battle held every first full weekend in March that puts history into a living, breathing context. Be prepared to take a lot of photos and videos.

Vistor Information

7502 Natural Bridge Road, Tallahassee, FL; (850) 487-7989; floridastateparks.org/parks-and-trails/natural-bridge-battlefield-historic-state-park; Call ahead for fees and hours.

FORT MOSE

Established: 1738
Location: Two miles north of St. Augustine
Decommissioned: The fort was abandoned in 1812

*S*panish Governor Manuel de Montiano established Fort Mose (pronounced Mosay) as the first free black settlement in the United States. The settlement around the fort that was populated by approximately 100 people was named Gracia Real de Santa Teresa de Mose.

In the late 1600s, asylum for slaves from British colonies was being offered by the Spanish government. In the eighteenth century, hundreds of thousands of African slaves were transported to the Carolinas to work on plantations. Realizing it needed to strengthen its force at St. Augustine, the Spanish government aided by Indian allies and other Africans helped escapees from the Carolinas and Georgia to settle in Fort Mose. That defended the northern approach to St. Augustine. Political alliances were formed with the Spanish and their Indian allies who fought against a common enemy.

The settlers lived in palm-thatched huts and cultivated indigo, corn, and citrus. Fish and shellfish such as oysters readily available on the fort's location on the small tidal channel named Mose Creek provided needed protein, as did nearby creeks of the North River which joins the Matanzas River to eventually form Matanzas Bay.

Able-bodied men either stood guard or patrolled the frontier. They also attended mass. There were a moat, earth walls smeared with clay, and wooden buildings within the fort. Shallow-draft Spanish boats were used to gather food and patrol creeks and rivers. The inhabitants' diet was in many respects like the indigenous Indians'.

In 1740 General James Oglethorpe attacked Fort Mose and captured it. Black militia, Spanish regular troops, and Indian auxiliaries counterattacked and defeated Oglethorpe, but Fort Mose was demolished in the process. The inhabitants of Fort Mose moved to St. Augustine while Oglethorpe departed and returned to Georgia. Two years later, Fort Mose had been rebuilt by the Spanish and resettled by most of the former slaves who had previously fled to the relative safety of St. Augustine.

In 1763 East Florida was ceded to the British in the Peace of Paris treaty, forcing most of the African inhabitants of Fort Mose to immigrate to Cuba along with Spanish settlers. The African population of Fort Mose and St. Augustine was estimated to be 3,000, of whom 75 percent were escaped slaves.

Visitor Information

Fort Mose Historic State Park, 15 Fort Mose Trail, St. Augustine, FL 32084, (904) 823-2232, floridaheritage.com/maritime/forts/

Fort Mose is located two miles north of St. Augustine, The 24-acre site is the premier site on the Florida Black Heritage Trail. Administered through the Anastasia State Recreation Area, it is also a Florida state park. Although nothing remains of Fort Mose, the land where the settlement was built is still visible.

The park is extremely user friendly. There is a nominal fee for adults to enter the visitor center. Children under six years of age are free. The visitor center is open Thursday through Monday from 9 a.m. to 5 p.m., and the grounds are open from 9 a.m. to 5 p.m. year-round. The visitor center has a film depicting the story of Fort Mose, administrative offices, air-conditioned restrooms, and audio and visual interactive exhibits including maps and paintings. Assistive listening devices are also available, as are large-print Florida Park Service publications. Several exhibits are in Braille. A sign language interpreter is also available. Pets are welcome but must be on a six-foot-long leash.

There are many opportunities for viewing bald eagles, white ibis, and great blue herons. The main boardwalk, restrooms, and visitor center/museum are wheelchair accessible. A manual wheelchair is available on a first-come, first-served basis.

There is interpretive visual signage on the park's main boardwalk. A second, floating boardwalk can be used to launch canoes and kayaks but only at high tide because it is on a tributary. Two picnic areas are available. One is near the main boardwalk; the other is behind the visitor center. Parking capacity can accommodate 26 vehicles.

If you are visiting the Castillo de San Marcos and/or Fort Matanzas in St. Augustine, a side trip to Fort Mose is well worth the effort.

FORT GEORGE

Established: 1763
Location: Pensacola
Decommissioned: 1781

*N*amed after King George and built by General
John Campbell, this British earth-and-wood fort surrounded by
a dry ditch was erected on Gage Hill 60 feet above the flood
level. Intended to protect Pensacola, it was vulnerable to attack
from even higher ground that lay to the northwest. Additional
fortifications named the Queen's Redoubt and the Prince of
Wales Redoubt were built to protect the fort. About 1,100 soldiers comprised the combined garrisons at any given time and
manned 20 embrasured guns on the parapet.

The fort was a quadrangle about 80 yards square and had
bastions at each corner. It was the headquarters of British West
Florida whose theater of operations went from the Suwannee
River to the Mississippi River. When the Spanish besieged the
fort, the Queen's Redoubt's magazine suffered a direct hit from
Spanish artillery in 1781, killing almost 100 defenders.

The Spanish General Bernardo de Galvez retook Pensacola
in May 1871 during the American Revolution and renamed
the fort San Miguel, but the Spanish also realized the fort was
indefensible and needed many repairs. It was never officially
occupied by the Spanish, who allowed it to deteriorate. During
the Civil War it was occupied by Union forces, who put a small

battery called Fort McClellan on the site, but it never engaged in combat.

Visitor Information

501 N. Palafox Street, Pensacola, FL 32501

The fort was added to the National Register of Historic Places in 1974, and a small portion of it has been reconstructed and is part of the Fort George, Memorial Park in the North Hill Preservation district.

Although there is no specific telephone number or website associated with Fort George, the modest reconstruction is well worth a visit. There are period cannons, a stockade wall, and ramparts on display.

Pensacola offers sugar-white beaches, a thriving visual arts scene, numerous museums, dolphin tours, and many other family-friendly cultural activities.

FORT BROOKE

Established: 1823
Location: Tampa
Decommissioned: 1883

*R*ecognizing the danger posed by the bellicose
Seminole Indians after Florida was acquired by the United
States from Spain, in 1823 the Department of the Army
ordered Colonels George Mercer Brooke and James Gadsden
to create a military manifestation on Tampa Bay that would
secure the area and project current military policy. As a result
of this order, four fully complemented companies of the United
States Fourth Infantry Regiment, comprised of approximately
600, presumably mounted, soldiers established Cantonment
Brooke at the mouth of the Hillsborough River on a chilly
January 10th. The site was (perhaps apocryphally) chosen due
to the presence of a majestic, enormous hickory tree standing
on top of an early Indian mound probably built by the Toco-
baga Indians hundreds of years before. The hickory tree was
chopped down, but several equally old oak trees were allowed
to remain to provide much-needed shade. The fort was constructed of logs and initially contained barracks, storehouses,
a blockhouse, guardhouse, powder magazine, stables, and a
wharf that accessed Garrison Channel.

At its height, the fort comprised 16 square miles. The
eastern boundary was where the Tampa Bay History Center
is today, and it was bordered on the west by what is now the

The Garrison at Fort Brook. Tampa, Florida.
FLORIDA MEMORY

Tampa Convention Center. An estimated 40,000 soldiers were intermittantly stationed at the fort during the Second Seminole War between 1835 and 1842. The fort was not to remain that large for long, because on July 25, 1848, Tampa was legally created. President Polk signed an Act of Congress that gave Hillsborough County 160 acres from Fort Brooke.

The soldiers conducted numerous mounted patrols against marauding Indians until January 10, 1861, when Florida seceded from the Union and the fort fell under the control of the Confederacy. The fort's garrison consisted of the Second Florida Infantry Battalion whose nominal strength was anywhere from 450 men to 700 men depending on the number of companies.

On October 16, 1963, two Union Navy ships, the USS *Tahoma* and the USS *Adela*, bombarded the fort and created a diversionary attack on Tampa. The *Tahoma* was an Unadilla class of gunboat that was oceangoing but had a shallow draft that enabled the ships to go into shallow waters. It displaced 691 tons, was 158 feet long and 28 feet at its beam, had a draft of only nine feet, six inches, had a crew of 114, and was powered by two 200-horsepower engines in addition to two sails. Its armament consisted of one 11-inch Dahlgren smoothbore cannon, two 24-pounder smoothbore cannon, and two 20-pounder Parrott rifles. Its top speed was 11.5 miles per hour or 10 knots.

Dalhgrens were designed by Rear Admirable John A. Dahlgren and saw wide use during the Civil War. Manufactured in many different sizes, their rounded, bulbous shapes, especially noticeable toward the rear of the gun, made them distinguishable from other cannons. The most used was the 11-inch, which weighed a whopping 15,700 pounds and could hurl with relative accuracy a 166-pound shell 3,650 yards or two miles.

These versatile guns were used both on ships and land. Because no Dahlgren shell ever exploded prematurely, they were obviously favored by their 10-man crews on ships and 11-man crews ashore. The shell guns could fire a variety of ammunition such as canister, shell, shrapnel, and grapeshot. The only Dahlgren model that could not fire grapeshot was the 15-inch shell gun.

The Parrott rifle was invented by Captain Robert Parker Parrott, U.S. Army, who became the superintendent of the West Point Foundry in Cold Spring, New York. These cast-iron cannons were known for their accuracy and came in sizes ranging from a 10-pounder to a rarely used 300-pounder. The largest gun used in the Civil War was the 20-pounder, but the 10-pounder was used more often and was manufactured in two bore sizes: 2.9-inch and 3.0-inch. The latter had a range of

2,000 yards or 1.1 miles. Parrott's gun tubes can be identified by the letters WPF (West Point Foundry) that are stamped along with a date between 1860 and 1889 on the front face of the tube. The Parrott rifles and the Dalhgrens were the cannon of choice for both Union and Confederate warships.

The *Adela* was the same class of boat, ideal for shallow-water work such as blockading. It displaced 585 tons, was 211 feet long, had a beam of 23 feet, six inches, and a draft of nine feet, three inches, and was powered by a side-wheeled steam engine. Its top speed was 14 miles per hour or 12 knots, and it was manned by 70 crew members and armed with four 24-pounder smoothbore cannon and two 20-pounder Parrott rifles. The ship was iron hulled.

The two ships had been tasked by Rear Admiral Theodorus Bailey to create a diversionary attack that would give cover to a land-based attack aimed at destroying two blockade runners loading cotton while sitting at anchor in the Hillsborough River.

Led by *Tahoma*'s commander, Lieutenant Commander Alexander A. Semmes, the two gunboats edged their way

Fort Brook. Circa 1900, Tampa, Florida.
FLORIDA MEMORY

toward the shore and when they were approximately 2,000 yards away began an earsplitting bombardment of the batteries that protected Tampa. The bombardment continued all day until the gunboats withdrew.

As soon as it was dark, 60 men from the *Tahoma* and 40 from the *Adela* rowed ashore in several small boats. Led by Acting Master T. R. Harris, they slogged and hacked their way through 14 miles of treacherous swamp to the Hillsborough River, where they found the two Confederate blockade runners, the steamer *Scottish Chief* and the sloop *Kate Dale*, riding at anchor. The two ships were owned by James McKay, the future mayor of Tampa.

The raiding party put the Confederate ships to the torch and headed back the same way they had come from, where small boats would pick them up and ferry them back to their ships. At their exfiltration point they were ambushed by soldiers from the 2nd Florida Infantry Battalion, and a violent firefight ensued. They were also attacked by Confederate cavalry, the Ocklawaha Rangers. The *Adela* provided covering fire, enabling the raiding party to row back to their ships and make their escape. The diversionary attack had created havoc in Tampa and resulted in the destruction of several Confederate ships including blockade runners and ships in dry-dock being repaired. Mission accomplished.

This was the only action in which Fort Brooke was involved. As the fort was gradually subsumed by the city of Tampa, soldiers' remains were reinterred at the Florida National Cemetery in Bushnell, while Indian remains were given to the Seminole Tribe of Florida. The last roll call was conducted in 1882 and the fort was decommissioned by the Army in 1883. In 1885, the fort became an unincorporated, independent town, and in 1907 it was annexed by Tampa. Artifacts were given to the Tampa Bay History Center. Tampa, officially established in

1848, is a thriving metropolis, the creation of which was due in no small part to Fort Brooke.

Visitor Information

Tampa Bay History Center, 801 Water Street, Tampa, FL 33602, (813) 228-0097, info@tampabayhistorycenter.org

Fort Brooke no longer exists. Commercial establishments in Ybor City and other parts of Tampa including part of an Interstate highway sit on top of what used to be the fort. Artifacts can be viewed at the Tampa Bay History Center.

FORT IZARD

Established: 1836
Location: Wakulla Springs
Decommissioned: 1865

*N*amed for First Lieutenant James F. Izard, 1st U.S. Dragoons, Fort Izard was established on February 27, 1836, and saw intermittent use until 1842. Izard was the first man killed at the fort after being struck by a lead bullet in his head from attacking Seminole Indians numbering 1,500 and led by Chiefs Osceola and Alligator. Osceola was later taken into custody at Fort Peyton, a wooden fort and blockhouse, while the Seminole chief was trying to negotiate a peace settlement under a white flag of truce in 1837. Peyton was established in 1837 on the south side of Moultrie Creek and was active for three years.

Fort Izard was built by troops under the command of General George P. Gaines who were attempting to cross the Withlacoochee River on their way to Fort Brooke in Tampa. When they came under attack, they constructed their fort but had to retreat to a hastily built, 250-yard-square quadrangle fortified by log breastworks and earth bastions.

A request was sent to Fort Clinch for reinforcements, but the siege lasted two weeks. After their regular rations were depleted, the men ate their horses and dogs. After two weeks the Seminoles requested a parlay, and during the talks 500 troops arrived and drove the Indians away. The fort was then abandoned.

If you like going to slightly out-of-the-way places and are fond of groups of keys or islands, Cedar Key, named for the ubiquitous eastern red cedar that once flourished there, will be right up your alley. Located 50 miles southwest of Gainesville, small and secluded Cedar Key is actually a cluster of islands at the edge of the Gulf of Mexico not far from the mouth of the Suwannee River.

The Cedar Keys were first utilized during the Second Seminole War. Troops occupied Atsena Otie key while Seminole captives were confined on nearby Seahorse Key before they were exiled to Oklahoma on what became known as the Trail of Tears.

By the time of the Civil War, a lighthouse, the lantern of which was 28 feet above the ground (the lighthouse sat on a 47-foot-high hill, putting the light 75 feet above sea level, enabling it to be seen from 16 miles away) had been erected on Seahorse Key and the improved harbor was bustling with small vessels.

There was also a desalination plant on Salt Key that created 160 bushels of salt daily. In March 1861, two months after Florida seceded from the Union and one month before Fort Sumter came under attack by Confederate forces, the Florida Railroad was completed. It formed a vital link between Cedar Key and Fernandina on the Atlantic side of the state. The railroad allowed vital materials to be shipped to Cedar Key.

The Confederates immediately fortified the valuable harbor, installing two 18-pounder cannons on Seahorse Key along with a barracks for the 4th Florida Infantry next to the railroad bridge to Cedar Key. Atsena Otie Key was also manned by troops armed with a 6-pounder field gun. It was from this key that two mills were producing cedar boards sent north to pencil factories. They also prudently turned off the lighthouse at Sea Horse Key and took away the supply of sperm oil used to light the lamp.

When it was thought that Union forces were planning an attack on Fernandina, reinforcements were sent from Cedar Key leaving it manned by only a handful of Confederate troops to protect it from the Union Navy.

At 10 a.m. on January 7, 1862, the USS *Hatteras* hove into view after having first stopped at Apalachicola, where it did a tour of blockade duty. The *Hatteras* was 1,126-ton steamer built at Harland and Hollingsworth in Wilmington, Delaware. It was commissioned in October 1861 at the Philadelphia Naval Yard, was 210 feet long, had a beam of 18 feet, and was propelled by a steam engine that powered two iron sidewheels allowing it to chug along at nine miles per hour. There were 126 men on board, and its armament consisted of four, 32-pounders and one 20-pounder.

Nine days after arriving at Cedar Key, the *Hatteras* went into action at about 10 a.m., attacking the railhead with sailors and Marines. Resistance by Confederate cavalry and civilian workers was stiff but brief. Before they made a strategic retreat to their ship, raiding Union forces came ashore and managed to obliterate buildings and railroad tracks. As it moved unmolested into the harbor's blue water, the *Hatteras* must have been an intimidating sight. It only fired three shots from its guns.

Not finished with their day's work, crew members either boarded, sank, or burned seven blockade runners, including the schooners *Anna Smith*, *Wyle*, and the *Aucilla*, which sat in Depot Key's harbor at the wharf, sending valuable cargos of cotton and turpentine to the bottom. The *Fanny* was lucky and managed to escape in the chaos by fleeing south along the coast to the Crystal River. Several fishing smacks were also burned. The raiders also captured 14 troops of the 22-man garrison, including the commanding officer. Harbor buildings on Seahorse Key were also put to the torch.

Approximately a year later, on January 6, 1863, the *Hatteras* joined the blocking group of ships led by Rear Admiral David Farragut who was endeavoring to gain control of the port of Galveston, Texas. Two days later, sails were seen on the horizon in the afternoon, and the *Hatteras* was ordered to give chase, which it did for four hours.

When it finally caught up with the square-rigged ship and demanded it identify itself, the mysterious ship claimed to be Her Majesty's Ship *Petrel*. Shortly after the commanding officer of the *Hatteras*, Captain Homer C. Blake, sent a longboat to inspect the ship, a different reply was yelled, and the ship identified itself as the CSS *Alabama*.

Its commander, Raphael Semmes, immediately opened fire with his cannon, and for about 20 minutes the two ships dueled. They were between 25 to 200 yards apart, and the gun flashes and thunder-like reverberations could be seen and heard by the Union squadron 16 miles away.

By the time the cruiser *Brooklyn* was sent to investigate, the *Hatteras* was on fire and sinking. Miraculously, only two of *Hatteras'* crew had been killed, and five were wounded. Six managed to board the ship's longboat and row to safety. Captain Blake and the rest of his crew were taken to Port Royal, Jamaica, and from there paroled back to the United States. Only two crew members of the *Alabama* were wounded.

Upon arriving on the scene, the following morning, the *Brooklyn* found the *Hatteras* vertical in the water about 20 miles south of Galveston Light. Only the sunken ship's masts could be seen above the water, but from the top mast the United States Navy commissioning pennant was fluttering in a light breeze.

Despite this victory, the Union forces did not occupy Cedar Key immediately, but they did return. The fighting was not over yet. Station Four was a stop on the railroad that went from

Cedar Key to Fernandina and was on the shore of Number Four Channel that divided Cedar Key from the mainland of Florida proper.

On February 9, Union Major Edmund C. Weeks led a column of 186 troopers attached to the 2nd Florida Cavalry and 200 soldiers belonging to the 2nd United States Colored Infantry off Cedar Key, where they headed to the interior of Florida, specifically Levy County. The smallish contingent then split into two separate columns. Major Benjamin Lincoln, who was leading the 2nd United States Colored Infantry, assaulted a rebel encampment located on the Suwannee River. At the same time Major Weeks and his men began the long trek back to Cedar Key.

Captain J. J. Dickison, the wily commander of the Confederate 2nd Florida Cavalry, initiated a series of hit-and-run attacks that eventually led to the battle of Station Four. Leading an assortment of soldiers from Company B from the 2nd Florida Cavalry, nearly a dozen men from the Special Battalion of Florida Cavalry, men assigned from the 1st Florida Reserves and troops from Company H of the 5th Florida Cavalry Dickison also had at his disposal a 12-pounder cannon.

What followed was chaos involving skirmishers on both sides, cavalry charges followed by dispersed retreats, cannon fire, whirring bullets, screaming orders from officers on both sides who tried to maintain a modicum of order and discipline, attacks and counterattacks and fighting involving small numbers of men on natural lands, the trestle, and the manmade railroad embankment. Casualties were relatively light on both sides.

The Union and Confederate commanders later gave different versions of the fight. Both sides claimed they withdrew for different reasons that allowed them to claim victory. The Battle of Station Four preceded the Battle of Natural Bridge.

Visitor Information

Cedar Key Museum State Park, 12231 SW 166th Court, Cedar Key, FL 32625, (352) 543-5350, floridastateparks.org/parks-and-trails/cedar-key-museum-state-park/experience

To commemorate this battle, the Cedar Key Museum State park was established in 1962.

FORT DALLAS

Established: 1837
Location: Miami River, Miami
Decommissioned: 1850

*F*ort Dallas was erected on a plantation owned by Richard Fitzpatrick and William English and was named in honor of Commodore Alexander James Dallas, who commanded the U.S. naval forces in the West Indies. Technically it was a containment, not a fortification, although there was a wooden stockade surrounding it.

Shortly after being occupied by both Army and Navy troops to protect settlers from hostile Seminole Indians the threat

Barracks from Fort Dallas at Brickell Point, Miami, Florida
FLORIDA MEMORY

dissipated, and the fort was abandoned. U.S. Marines briefly occupied the fort until the Army took up residence during the Civil War. William H. English used the empty fort as the basis for a village he called Miami. Nothing remains of the fort.

Visitor Information

Fort Dallas Park, 64 Se 4th St, Miami, FL 33131, (305) 416-1416

FORT DULANEY

Established: 1837
Location: Punta Rassa
Decommissioned: 1858

*F*ort Delaney was a U.S. Army supply depot tasked with shipping cattle south to the Union troops stationed in Key West. The fort also had a hospital. Its first iteration only lasted one year and was abandoned in 1838. It was reoccupied in 1841 so it could hold Seminole prisoners before they were sent to the Indian Territories. A hurricane destroyed the fort in October 1841.

The Army then moved up the Caloosahatchee River to Fort Harvie, which in turn was abandoned in 1842 and subsequently morphed into Fort Myers that eventually became a thriving city of the same name.

Although of little military significance, it is another example of how the geographic location of some seemingly innocuous forts led over a period of relatively few years to the establishment of more permanent sites.

Visitor Information

Punta Rassa, SR 867, South Side of the Punta Rassa River, Located in Punta Rassa Florida. Little remains of the town.

Hiking trails give birders the opportunity to see roseate spoonbills, American avocets, and white ibis at low tide while the

*Barracks built by the U.S. government during the Seminole War (1825)
under General Winfield Scott Hancock, This building housed the farthest
south cable station from 1866 to 1906 when the building burned.*
FLORIDA STATE ARCHIVES.

tidal marshes are great for paddling, but the canoe and kayak
launching place is unimproved and does require a portage.
Mockingbirds, blue jays, doves, hammering woodpeckers, and
twitchy gray squirrels also call the park home. If you're really
lucky you'll spot a thumb-size green tree frog and the obviously
larger and easier to see but just as reclusive gopher tortoises.

Native Florida vegetation such as sand pine, slash pine,
southern red cedar, oak, sabal palm, wax myrtle, saw palmetto,
coontie and yaupon holly proliferate. Restrooms are near the
museum and are wheelchair accessible, as is the museum. A
wheelchair is available on a first-come, first-served basis to park
visitors. Bring your dog but keep it on a six-foot-long leash. You
cannot leave it unattended for longer than 30 minutes nor can
you bring it into the museum. Informative literature and depic-
tions are available. Some of the guns originally on Sea Horse

Key are on display. There is a diorama depicting the Battle of Station Four plus artifacts.

A second museum, the Cedar Key Historical Society Museum at 7070 D Street, contains exhibits and photographs and also information about the Battle of Station Four. Outside are kettles used to extract salt from nearby saline water.

The scenery on Cedar Key is drop-dead gorgeous. Bear in mind that summer months in Florida can be quite hot and humid, but visitors tend to be fewer. At sites near or on the water like Cedar Key the heat is often mitigated by breezes. Afternoon thunderstorms accompanied by potentially dangerous lightening are not uncommon. Conversely winter months are obviously dryer and cooler, there are usually more visitors, and breezes coming off the water can be brisker.

Cedar Key's charm is enhanced by its somewhat out-of-the-way location. Activities abound, and park rangers are knowledgeable and happy to share information. Don't be afraid to ask questions. The community of Cedar Key is less than 1,000 but vibrant and well worth visiting. The key itself is only 10 feet above sea level and there are camping opportunities on neighboring keys. If you want to visit a historical site and get away from it all, this is the place for you.

FORT MCREE

Established: 1837
Location: Perdido Key, Pensacola, Florida
Decommissioned: 1947

*I*t took three years to build Fort McCree at Foster's Bank on the eastern end of what is known today as Perdido Key. Designed by the Frenchman Simon Bernard, the fort was three-tiered with a separate water battery near to sea level. There will be a separate chapter on Simon Bernard and the contributions he made to coastal fortifications.

Pensacola Bay is 13 miles long by only 2.5 miles wide. The northern portion of the bay is seven feet, six inches, deep, and the southern portion is 19 feet, eight inches, deep. Other islands include Robertson Island, Sand Island, and White Island.

Shaped like a boomerang because it was located on a small, narrow barrier island, McCree nevertheless boasted a formidable and intimidating 19 casements. Four were on each side, one was on the tip, and five were placed on each wing. Each casement had the capability of accommodating four cannons.

Bernard made a slight variation. Quarters and storerooms occupied eight casements, and two of the eight were the powder magazines that measured 17 by 35 feet in area. Although this meant that the wings were underdefended, 44 casement cannon of either 8-inch or 6-inch caliber were still aimed at Pensacola Pass, more than enough to stop enemy ships from venturing too close. The fort could when fully armed boast of 122 guns, although all of these guns weren't installed until 1843 to 1845. When the Civil War began, Fort McCree had 15 smoothbore, muzzle-loading Columbiads, the largest and heaviest form of artillery available at the time.

The first iterations of cast-iron Columbiads were cast in 1811 and featured a 7.25-inch bore and fired a 50-pound projectile. It took more than 30 years of development before an 8-inch and a 10-inch model became widely available. The 8-inch version weighed a hefty 9,240 pounds and could hurl a 65-pound shell 4,400 yards or 2.5 miles and a solid short projectile slightly farther, 4,800 yards or 2.7 miles.

The 10-inch Columbiad weighed a whopping 15,400 pounds and could fire a 128-pound shell 4,800 yards and a solid shot 5,600 yards or 3.1 miles. The massively heavy and cumbersome guns crewed by 14 men that could fire in both low and high trajectories were supported on seacoast carriages and recoiled slightly up inclined wood beams. There was also a traversing rail that allowed the cannon to swing slightly from left to right. Typically, the arc was less than 180 degrees, but some batteries could swing in a full circle.

There were two other types built. A 15-inch Columbiad tipped the scales at over 25 tons and could hurl a 400-pound projectile 5,000 yards. At over double the weight, over 60 tons, a 20-inch model could fire a shell over five miles. None of these larger models were used during the Civil War, and very few were ever built. When fired, the noise created by these monster guns was deafening.

Just before the war an improved version of Columbiads was developed by Ordnance Corps officer Thomas Jackson Rodman. The guns that bore his name were designed to reduce cracking, because the iron cooled evenly from the inside out.

This process enabled larger-bore Columbiads to be cast in northern foundries.

Many Columbiads and a lesser number of Rodmans remained at seacoast fortifications after the war and along with Parrott rifles and recoilless rifles are the ones most visitors see. They are also on display at state and national parks. Rodmans are very similar in appearance to Columbiads but tend to be bigger. These guns represent the acme of smoothbore cannons but were made obsolete by the advent of rifled cannons.

The 12-foot-wide sally port was on the walls facing land and were called the gorge that was designed to contain six casements capable of mounting one cannonade. The gorge had six casements of which three on either side were used as living quarters. Together with its sister forts Pickens across Pensacola Pass on Santa Rose Island and Barrancas also across Pensacola Bay on what is now the Naval Air Station Pensacola, it guarded the entrance to Pensacola Bay.

Fort McCree was named after Army engineer Colonel William McCree, who distinguished himself in the War of 1812 and later studied fortification design in France and Belgium. In 1819, McCree resigned from the Army in protest of the naming of Simon Bernard as assistant chief engineer of the Corps of Engineers.

Although there was not a shortage of cannon men, they were at a premium. On December 1, 1853, the entire strength of the U.S. Army was reported to be 10,417, requiring commanding officers to be very judicious in the placement of their available assets.

At the conclusion of the Mexican-American War in 1848 Fort McCree was manned only during target practice, drills, and maneuvers. Barracks had been built at nearby Fort Barrancas on the mainland. The first men stationed at Fort McCree were from the First Company, Third Artillery, and they arrived on May 2, 1845.

Faced with being in the unenviable and untenable position of having to occupy all three Pensacola forts with a paltry 50 men, ranking officer First Lieutenant Adam J. Slemmer prudently decided to assemble his miniscule force on Fort Barrancas. This was a temporary move. After spiking the guns at Forts McCree and Barrancas, Lieutenant Slemmer moved again to more secure ground at Fort Pickens on January 10, the day Florida seceded from the Union. Forts McCree and Barrancas were now in Confederate hands.

The move was prescient, because two days later, on January 12, the Florida and Alabama militia came on the scene and occupied the two evacuated forts. In the ensuing months more personnel were added by both the Union and Confederacy. New batteries were built by both sides. They engaged in a series of earsplitting cannon duels that had little substantial effect. In the 12 months that followed, the Confederates had a manpower advantage over the Union forces of about 7,000 to 2,000.

Pensacola was in Confederate hands commanded by General Braxton Bragg, a West Point-educated general who had seen action in the Second Seminole War and the Mexican-American War. By most accounts Bragg was argumentative and disrespectful of authority and is regarded as being one of the least effective Confederate generals. On October 9, 1861, Bragg ordered an attack on Fort Pickens. The attack failed. The commander of the Union forces, Colonel Harvey Brown at Fort Pickens, planned a counterattack on Fort McCree because it was the closest fort to Fort Pickens and a barrier to any future attack on Pensacola itself.

Aided by two ships, the *Niagara* and the *Richmond*, Union forces at Fort Pickens bombarded Fort McCree on the morning of November 22, 1861. The Confederates briefly returned fire but by the end of the day had been overwhelmed and their guns fell silent.

The *Niagara* was a steam frigate propelled by both sails and a steam engine that belched streams of black smoke from its two funnels amidships. It displaced 5,629 tons, was 328 feet, 10 inches long, had a beam of 55 feet, four inches, and a complement of 251 officers and other crew members and was armed with 12 11-inch Dahlgren smoothbore guns. It was also relatively new, having been launched by the New York Navy Yard on February 23, 1855, and commissioned on April 6, 1857.

The *Richmond* was also new, having been launched in January 1860 and commissioned the same year. Propelled by a steam engine, the *Richmond* was capable of chugging along at 10 miles per hour or nine knots. It displaced 2,604 tons, was 225 feet long, had a beam of 42 feet, six inches, a draft of 17 feet, four inches, and was manned by 259 officers and enlisted men. Its armament consisted of one 80-pounder Dahlgren smoothbore gun, 20 9-inch Dahlgren smoothbore guns and one 30-pounder Parrott rifle. It received a hit from one of McCree's guns four feet underwater on its starboard side, causing serious leaks and forcing it to return to Key West for needed repairs.

Fort McCree's commander, Colonel John B. Villepigue, advised General Bragg that his position was untenable and requested permission to sabotage the fort and withdraw his men. His request was denied.

At mid-morning of November 23, the assault on McCree resumed. The combined guns from the *Niagara* and Fort Pickens methodically bludgeoned McCree to death. Huge gaps in the protective walls were created while other parts of the wall were completely blown away and other sections collapsed. Flames engulfed wood decking in the fort's interior, and one powder magazine caved in.

When the Confederates left Pensacola, they burned Fort McCree in a final act of defiance. But the fort refused to die. It remained in its derelict state for 30 years. Two jetties were built to mitigate beach erosion. Fifty thousand bricks were removed in 1875 and were used to make walkways and repairs at Fort Barrancas.

Fort McCree continued to exist. To the west of the fort in 1898 a battery of two 8-inch rifled guns was built and was named Battery Slemmer. A year later a battery of rapid-fire guns was installed and named Battery Center. They were manned by between 50 and 100 members of the U.S. Army Coast Artillery Corps that rotated in and out from Fort Barrancas.

A hurricane with sustained winds of 85 miles per hour and a storm surge of 12 feet above normal high tide that hit Fort McCree on September 26 and 27 flattened most of the newer buildings that had been put in place since 1898. In 1911 a sea-wall 11 feet high, with a bottom width of 13 feet and a top width of five feet, was completed.

The guns of Battery Slemmer were sent to Europe to aid America's entry into World War I and mounted on railway cars. The guns at Battery Center were regarded as surplus and also removed. McCree was abandoned once again.

A battery named Battery 233 of two 6-inch shield guns with a range of 15 miles was planned because of the start of World War II. Carriages were received and foundations were laid, but the war ended before the guns were put in place and that was Fort McCree's swan song.

In 1971, the U.S. Navy, which had been managing Forts McCree, Barrancas, and Pickens turned them over to the National Park Service where they became part of the Gulf Islands National Seashore. Fort McCree's service had finally come to an end after almost 140 years.

Visitor Information

Gulf Island National Sea Shore, nps.gov

There is no specific address, telephone number, or website associated with Fort McCree. Little remains of the fort because it is
underwater. Snorkelers can glimpse vague outlines of the fort's
structures. There are no visitor facilities at the site. The use
of metal detectors is against the law, as is the removal of any
artifacts.

FORT JUPITER

Established: January 25, 1838
Location: Jupiter
Decommissioned: 1842

*F*ort Jupiter was built on a point of land called Pennock Point three miles west of the Jupiter Inlet during the Second Seminole War by General Thomas S. Jessup and held more than 600 captured Seminoles before they were taken to Fort Brooke and later to Indian Territory in Oklahoma. It was closed in 1842, reopened in the 1850s, and closed for good when the war ended.

Visitor Information

Loxahatchee River Battlefield Park, 9060 Indian River Road, Jupiter, FL 33478, (561) 741-1359

There were two minor battles on the Loxahatchee River in January 1838, and these are commemorated in the Loxahatchee River Battlefield Park. Admission is free. The park is open from sunrise to sunset and comprises 61.64 acres. There are picnic areas, 10 miles of nature trails, seven miles of horse trails, and five miles of waterway trails. Dogs are allowed, but they must be on a six-foot-long leash. A picturesque community is named after the fort.

Jupiter is part of the Palm Beach area, a well-known tourist destination with numerous lighthouse views and affordable accommodations.

FORT LAUDERDALE

Established: March 1838
Location: Fort Lauderdale
Decommissioned: May 1838

*M*arching south from Fort Jupiter with four companies (approximately 400 soldiers) Major William Lauderdale arrived at the New River on March 5, 1838, and promptly built a double-tired blockhouse surrounded by a larger picket. Failing to find and engage Seminole Indians the fort was vacated two months later.

During the Third Seminole War it was reoccupied from 1856 to 1857 before being abandoned as too swampy and virtually uninhabitable. In 1924 Coast Guard Base Six was established.

Visitor Information

There is no address, telephone number, or website associated with Fort Lauderdale. A development now sits on the original site. The fort is an excellent example of the interconnectivity of the previous two forts and how they interacted and depended on one another. Enlistment periods were six months, which meant that troops were rotating in and out on a semiyearly basis.

These forts were basically temporary structures meant to give their occupants maximum protection with minimum effort put into construction. Many of the forts were built during the winter months that are obviously cooler thus sparing the men, at least temporarily, from the demanding conditions they would soon face. Today a city bears the name of the once-derelict fort.

Ft. Lauderdale is known for luxury hotels, boating canals including gondola rides, upscale restaurants, and a historic waterfront.

FORT PIERCE

Established: 1838
Location: Fort Pierce
Decommissioned: 1842

*F*ort Pierce was the primary supply depot for the U.S. Army during the Second Seminole War and was named after its first commander, Lieutenant Colonel Benjamin Kendrick Pierce. After making a lengthy reconnaissance of the area Pierce and his men settled on a site on December 31 at the Indian River Inlet where there was evidence the Spanish had built a fort around 100 years prior. Two days later a sturdy blockhouse made of palmetto logs was constructed high on a bluff.

On January 15 Brigadier General Thomas Sidney Jesup, known as the Father of the Modern Quartermaster Corps due to his 52-year service, having been appointed Quartermaster General by President James Monroe on May 8, 1818, moved in with his staff. Fort Pierce was known as Headquarters, Army of the South. As befitting the Quartermaster Corps, fish, oysters, and game were plentiful around the fort and easily obtained. The men ate well.

The Corps left Fort Pierce in 1842 at the conclusion of the Second Seminole War and was, like other forts, burned to the ground the following year.

Visitor Information

South Indian River Drive (at County Road 707), Fort Pierce, FL 34950

Nothing remains of Fort Pierce today. Fort Pierce is yet another example of how a military installation morphed into a town and later a prosperous city.

FORT MYERS

Established: 1850
Location: Fort Myers
Decommissioned: 1863

*E*stablished on February 20, 1850, by Major Samuel C. Ridgely where Fort Harvie once stood and named for Captain Abraham C. Myers who just happened to be the son-in law of Major General David E. Twiggs who ordered the fort built, Fort Myers had more than 50 buildings including officers' quarters, administration offices, houses for supplies and munitions, guardhouse, kitchen, bakery, laundry, sutler's store, stables, a two-and-a-half-story hospital, bowling alley, a 1,000-foot wharf and a pavilion. The fort was on a well-used road that led from Fort Brooke to Fort Pierce and is an example of the number of basically temporary installations that were constructed to serve a specific need.

After the Third Seminole War ended in 1856, the fort was abandoned two years later in June 1858. During the Civil War, the fort was reoccupied in December 1863 and manned by three companies, approximately 300 officers and men and was the only federally occupied fort in south Florida. The 2nd Florida Cavalry, the 110th New York Volunteer Infantry, and a company or about 100 men from the Second United States Colored Infantry both of whom were from Fort Zachary Taylor in Key West. In addition, more than 400 civilians occupied the fort during the Union reoccupation.

Under the command of Captain James Doyle, new barracks were built, as was a log-and-earth breastwork that surrounded the fort. The mission of the soldiers was to raid Confederate cattle ranchers operating in a large area north of the Caloosahatchee River in order to seize herds of cattle from smallholdings thereby disrupting valuable and needed beef shipments to the Confederate Army of Tennessee in Georgia. Like Fort Mose, it also served as a sanctuary for escaped slaves.

Beef supplies were a critical component to the Confederate war effort. Florida was and still is to a great extent a beef-producing state. To counter the Union raids and to protect the shipments the Confederates created a battalion of state militia commanded by Colonel C. J. Munnerlyn that was comprised of cattle drovers who were excused from regular service in the Confederate Army. This quasi-military unit was known as the Cattle Guard Battalion or Cow Cavalry.

Based at Fort Meade in February 1865, the Confederates totaling three companies, approximately 300 men give or take a few, and one artillery piece arrived at old Fort Thompson in what is now LaBelle, slogged down the river, and the following morning attacked Fort Myers, surprising a handful of black Union soldiers who were on picket duty.

Colonel Munnerlyn arrogantly fired one shot from his cannon at the fort that was now on high alert and brazenly demanded Captain Doyle's surrender. No doubt incensed the Union commander promptly refused and in an act of defiance wheeled out his own two cannon manned by black soldiers while his white cavalrymen peppered the enemy with bullets fired from their carbines that were either a Burnside model or a breech-loading, metallic-rim fire cartridge Frank Wesson. Both models were issued to Union cavalry during the war.

Sporadic fighting continued throughout the day. Nightfall brought an end to the action. Although they probably knew the importance of their mission, the Confederate Cow Cavalry recoiled under the sound of Union bullets and the following morning the Confederate forces left. The fort was permanently abandoned in June 1865.

On February 21, 1865, Captain Manuel A. Gonzalez arrived at the fort. Having delivered mail and supplies to the fort during the Seminole Wars and the Civil War, Gonzalez was familiar with the area. His wife Evalina and daughter Mary, along with Joseph Vivas and his wife Christiana Stirrup Vivas, came. Gonzalez and his family settled near the old fort and established a trading post thus founding the community of Ft. Myers.

This fort, like other posts and cantonments, including Fort Meade, did not engage in any major battles, nor was it commanded by officers who achieved any notoriety or fame. Nevertheless, it is an example of how either by accident or design a modest military installation can almost inadvertently be the genesis of a much larger and well-known entity that exists today.

Visitor Information

There is no specific address, telephone number or website associated with Fort Myers as nothing remains.

FORT DADE

Established: 1906
Location: Mullet Key, Tampa
Decommissioned: 1923

*F*ort Dade was named after Major Francis L. Dade, 4th U.S. Infantry who was killed along with his entire command by Seminole Indians on December 28, 1835. This coastal defense fort boasted two 109-man artillery barracks, officers' quarters, hospital, mess hall, administration building, guard house and later added a gym, NCO (noncommissioned officers such as sergeants and corporals) quarters, fire station, and a power plant. The fort was a training camp during World War I, and although it had been decommissioned, it served as a U-boat lookout post and bombing practice range during World War II.

Most of the buildings have been destroyed, but on the edge of the beach are two 8-inch disappearing guns. In 1974, the key was designated a National Wildlife Refuge. There are gopher tortoises, hummingbirds, and seabirds on the key but food, water, and restrooms are not available. No pets or alcoholic beverages are permitted.

Visitor Information

Egmont Key State Park, 4905 34th Street South #5000, St. Petersburg, FL 33711, (727) 709-0088, floridastateparks.org/perks-and-trails/egmont-key-state-park

Edmont Key State Park, Tampa, Florida
FLORIDA STATE PARKS

Fort Dade is part of the Egmont Key State Park. Egmont Key is accessible only by ferry or private boat and is southwest of Fort de Soto Park, which is on nearby Mullet Key. Egmont Key is also a state park and was named after John Percival, the Second Earl of Egmont and a member of the Irish House of Commons.

The park is free, but the south end is a shorebird refuge for osprey, brown pelicans, white ibis, royal and sandwich terns, black skimmers, American oystercatchers and laughing gulls. Pets are not allowed on Egmont Key but fishing in designated areas only is permitted. Sea trout, grouper, snapper, and tarpon have been known to be caught. All fishing must conform to regulations regarding size, number, how the fish is caught, and season.

There are six miles of paths along which gopher tortoises and Florida box turtles can be seen on occasion. Picnic tables are available on the north end of the island. Snorkeling is quite popular, as is sunbathing on the sugar white beaches. There are no restrooms. Although slightly out of the way, Egmont Key offers views and serenity that make it well worth a visit.

FORT DE SOTO

Established: 1906
Location: Egmont Key, Tampa
Decommissioned: 1910

*T*he fort was named for the Spanish explorer Hernando de Soto and was officially a sub post of nearby Fort Dade. There are four 12-inch M 1890-M1, breech-loading, rifled mortars made at Watervliet Arsenal in Watervliet, New York, on display, the only examples in North America. Also, of interest are two 6-inch British rapid-fire rifles manufactured by the W. B. Armstrong Company of England. None of the guns were ever fired in anger.

This uniquely situated fort is home to unique examples of cannons.

Designed to protect the entrance to Tampa Bay, construction on this rectangular, Spanish-built fort began in 1898 and ended in 1903. It boasts the only remaining examples of 12-inch breech-loading, rifled mortars in the United States. It is located eight miles south of St. Petersburg on Mullet Key.

Visitor Information

Fort de Soto Park, 3500 Pinellas Bayway S., Tierra Verde, FL 33715, (727) 582-2100, pinellascounty.org/parks

Fort de Soto Park Canon
© JIMVALLEE/GETTY IMAGES

Like Fort Dade this fort on Mullet Key eight miles south of St. Petersburg is accessible only by ferry or private boat and is within view of Fort Dade that lies just across a narrow channel.

There is a free history museum and interpretative maps that show where 29 buildings once stood. There are also brick roads, concrete sidewalks, and a narrow-gauge railroad used to move materials around the key. The guns still face out to sea and were the first lines of defense for Tampa. For the men subjected to harsh physical conditions serving at Fort Dade and Fort de Soto, it must have been very lonely.

Egmont Key is 450 acres, and approximately 250 soldiers were stationed there while Mullet Key, 1,136 acres, had half as many. Union soldiers were stationed there during the Civil War.

There is a plethora of activities available on visitor-friendly Mullet Key including two long piers with bait-and-tackle and food concessions, picnic areas, a museum., two swimming areas, nature trail, a seven-mile multipurpose trail, snack bar, gift shop, an 800-foot-long boat ramp, camping area for tents and RVs with a store, restrooms and laundry room, a 2.4-mile-long canoe trail, and Paw Playground, a designated area for pets.

Located south of and within easy striking distance of Tampa, St. Petersburg is one of the prettier cities on the west coast of Florida. In addition to miles of pristine beaches, it has a small-town feel that many find appealing.

FORGOTTEN FORTS

There were literally dozens of inland, coastal, or riverine blockhouses, cantonments, and forts scattered throughout the interior and along the sides of Florida's long peninsula and what is known as the Panhandle where the state swings to the west and terminated in Pensacola. Many have histories accessible only in arcane, hard-to-find official Army records while others have left indelible marks that remain to this day. Some are remembered only by commemorative plaques or statues, while others have towns and cities that bear their name. Here is a small, representative sampling.

Camp Deposit: Built in 1841, the camp is situated in the Big Cypress Swamp.

Camp Edgefield: Five miles southwest of Summer Haven. Camp Edgefield was built in 1836 and used for only two days.

Camp Jackson: A Confederate fort west of Jacksonville that was in service for the year of 1864.

Camp Pinckney: In service for the year of 1864 as a Confederate fort on Little Front Creek near the St. Mary's River.

Everglades Post: Survived the year of 1857 in the Everglades.

Fort Cross: Erected in 1857, Fort Cross is four miles northwest of Fort Poinsett.

Fort Doane: Erected more than 10 years before Fort Simon Drum, two miles west of Lake Trafford in 1841 and was closed a year later.

Fort Foster: Located nine miles north of Naples toward Immokalee, occupied from 1837 to 1838.

Fort Fulton: Constructed in 1840 on Pelicier Creek near the Matanzas Inlet.

Fort Hanson: Built in 1840 at the headwaters of Deep Creek, 13 miles southwest of St. Augustine.

Fort Hogtown: Located in Gainesville, a local militia fort built in 1817. Hogtown was the original name of Gainesville.

Fort Howell: 10 miles east of inland Everglades City and built in 1835 lasted only the year.

Fort Jacksonville: A settlers' log blockhouse used from 1836 to 1851. Today Jacksonville is one of Florida's largest cities.

Fort Keals: Located 10 miles south of Immokalee and had a longer term of service from 1838 to 1857.

Fort Kissimmee: Survived the years 1850–1857 and is the namesake of the city of Kissimmee.

Fort Ogden: Established in 1841 on the site of a Seminole Indian fort. Ogden was tasked with being an advance post for the "Big Cypress Campaign" and was later abandoned. A city now bears its name.

Fort Picolata and Fort San Francisco de Pupo: Across from each other on the St. Johns River on an old Indian crossing, Picolata was built in 1700 and was in existence for approximately 13 years while Pupo was built four years later and was abandoned approximately 69 years later. Both were British forts and were demolished in 1740 by the Georgia colonial militia in 1740. In 1743, the British rebuilt them and made them more defendable as 30-foot two-story square coquina towers that had eight guns each and were moated and palisaded. After 1763 British troops occupied them sporadically.

Fort Poinsett: In Cape Sable, Fort Poinsette functioned from 1838 to 1842.

Fort Santa Lucia de Canaveral: A Spanish fort erected in 1568. Because indigenous Indians killed so many of the troops there, they mutinied and fled to St. Augustine. Canaveral in Spanish means "reed bed" or "sugar cane plantation." Canaveral is the third oldest European place-name in the United States. San Juan, Puerto Rico is the second. Canaveral is now a thriving city and the launching site for NASA spacecraft.

Fort Shackleford: Operational for 1 year, Fort Shackleford was located 20 miles from the south shore of Lake Okeechobee and was operational for one year.

Fort Shannon: A large U.S. Army Quartermaster Depot built in Palatka and occupied from 1848 to 1843. The fort had stables for 400 horses, a hospital, barracks and eight block-houses. Prior to being a fort, the site was a trading post in 1821 that was burned by Seminoles in 1836.

Fort Simon Drum: A stockade depot between Immokalee and Lake Trafford. Troops served there from 1855 to 1856.

Fort Winder: Established in 1852 on the Peace River two miles from Fort Ogden.

Key Biscayne Post: Located in the present-day city of the same name. It was built in 1838 and renamed Fort Bankhead in 1838 and a year later was renamed Fort Russell. From 1842 to 1844 the U.S. Navy occupied the post. The U.S. Army rotated occupancy from Key Biscayne and Fort Dallas (Miami) from 1838 to 1842

FLORIDA'S LASTING CATHEDRALS OF WAR

*C*haracterized by thick walls that could easily withstand bombardments from land or sea and bristling with the biggest and most powerful cannons available at the time all of these fortifications were, at the time of their construction the most important military structures in the New World.

These iconic forts are must-see destinations and will more than satisfy a variety of interests. All of them are marvelously preserved and are almost completely intact and the views from their two- and three-story ramparts are uniformly spectacular. Many period-correct cannon of different sizes and calibers still sit where they were originally placed. Similarly, the perspective when standing at the base of their vertical walls gives an entirely different view and conveys perhaps more accurately the sheer mass and bulk of the structures. Each of these structures was designed to serve a specific purpose and all are unique, one-of-a-kind examples.

Expansive, verdant areas typically surround these fortifications, offering visitors the opportunity to picnic or take leisurely strolls. Many of the forts have been incorporated into the national park system and offer educational ranger-guided tours. Informational brochures are also available, and most of the forts have attached museums that contain fascinating minutia relevant to the fort. Because they are so large, visitors are encouraged to take their time in exploring the forts and their adjacent facilities.

Photo and video opportunities at all these forts are endless. Full-service amenities often include restrooms, hiking trails, wildlife viewing, and gift shops. Boating and fishing are sometimes available, depending on the location. All the fortifications comply with the Americans with Disabilities Act. There is ample parking. In most if not all the forts, well-behaved, leashed dogs are welcome. Entrance fees vary, but usually children under a certain age are not charged an admission fee. Interpretive centers are the rule, not the exception.

In or near large cities, the forts also offer visitors a chance to avail themselves of the variety of cultural activities and sightseeing such large cities afford. The obvious exception is Fort Jefferson in the Dry Tortugas, equidistant between Key West, Florida, and Havana, Cuba. Intrepid visitors can reach Fort Jefferson from Key West by high-speed catamaran, private vessel, or seaplane. Although not particularly large in terms of either population or land area, Key West had its own idiosyncratic set of charms and interests that appeal to a wide spectrum of visitors from all walks of life.

Most Third System forts were based on a hexagon shape because of the limits of casement cannon carriages and how big the embrasures were. The cannon could not move laterally more than 60 degrees, which meant that contiguous fort fronts had to meet at an angle of 120 degrees at a minimum. If they did not, there would be dead spaces in the target area.

In alphabetical order, here is your guide to Florida's coastal fortifications.

BATTERY SAN ANTONIO

AN ADDITIONAL DETERRENT TO
AN EXISTING FORTIFICATION

*C*onstructed in Pensacola between 1773 and 1797, this half-circle-shaped, Spanish-built, water-level, three-gun battery, also known as the Spanish Water Battery or the Battery of Saint Anthony in English, complemented the much larger Fort Barrancas that loomed above it.

The battery's purpose was to give its guns maximum field of fire on ships entering Pensacola Bay. The main advantage of a water battery was that because the battery was almost at water level, cannonballs aimed at ships could skip over the water much like stones.

Its first iteration was British and was named the Royal Navy Redoubt. Then the Spanish took control of it and abutting Fort Barrancas (much more on that later) and finally, on July 17, 1821, it became an American possession.

Oddly enough, it highly resembles a battery of the same name that was in the city of Algeciras, Spain. That battery aided in the defense of the city during the siege of Gibraltar and was an integral part of the entire defensive system designed by Jorge Próspero de Verboom. The battery itself was designed in 1743 by Salvador Palau and was situated on the cliffs overlooking the city. Horseshoe-shaped it had a circular parapet and two lateral parapets surrounded by a moat. The guns, powder keg–filled, wooden magazine, and a warehouse were behind the parapet.

The American version was designed by William Henry Chase, who at the time was a Florida militia colonel who had graduated from the U.S. Military Academy and served in the U.S. Corps of Engineers from 1815 to 1856. Chase also designed Fort Pickens while he was a captain, and it was he who demanded the surrender of the fort.

In 1839, a rear wall was added to the existing masonry battery, 13 cannons were placed on the ramparts, and infantry housing was built as well as places from which infantrymen could fire muskets. The battery was then named the Spanish Water Battery.

Considering when it was first completed and counting the additions made over the years and the number of times it changed hands, the Battery San Antonio is regarded as being the third-oldest standing fortification in Florida and one of the oldest in the continental United States.

The steps leading to the top of the rampart are quite steep and require a certain amount of physical exertion, but the expansive views are well worth it.

Visitor Information

Battery San Antonio, 3182 Taylor Road, Pensacola, FL 32508, nps.gov

Fort Barrancas and Battery San Antonio are under the auspices of the Gulf Islands National Seashore. Check website for fees and hours.

BRITISH FORT AT PENSACOLA

THE BRITISH STRUGGLE TO KEEP PACE WITH SPAIN

*I*n 1793 British troops occupied the existing Spanish fort (Fort Barrancas) that was subsequently enlarged, expanded, and made more defensible by the creation of bastions and a dry moat.

The Spanish were there first. In 1698, they established the Presidio Santa Maria de Galve, the first European settlement in Pensacola, near present-day Fort Barrancas. In addition to a neighboring village, the presidio also included Fort San Carlos de Austria.

San Carlos de Austria was a star fort with pine log walls that were laid horizontally across posts driven into the ground. Their gaps were filled with sand, and they were about 10 feet high and surrounded by a three-foot-deep moat.

Inside the fort were a hospital, warehouse, church, governor's residence and separate barracks for officers, regular soldiers, and convict laborers. Because there were no brick kilns or a local source for stones, all the buildings were wood. Initially the walls and roofs were made of palmetto thatch, but they were gradually replaced by lead sheeting or shingles and plank walls were added to the more important buildings. Extreme humidity rotted the horizontally placed logs, and by 1707 they had been replaced by vertical ones. Thus began the long and often-tumultuous journey of what was eventually to become Fort Barrancas.

In 1719, Fort San Carlos de Austria was destroyed by the French and thus a tug-of-war ensued that saw the Royal Navy Redoubt built under British rule in 1763. Twenty-four years later, Spain controlled the fort and built the Battery de San Antonio. For good measure, a wood-and-earth structure called Fort San Carlos de Barrancas was built. Barrancas are the red clay bluffs that overlook Pensacola Bay. Before that, in 1754 the Spanish had built the Presidio San Miguel de Panzacola, from which Pensacola took its name.

Spain and Britain who both knew the strategic importance of the fort in its relationship to Pensacola Bay continued to battle over possession of the fort. In 1763 they built the Royal Navy Redoubt where Fort Barrancas sits today.

During the War of 1812, Fort Barrancas was demolished by the British after they evacuated it because Andrew Jackson advanced on Pensacola on November 6, 1814, with 3,000 soldiers. Some Indians allied themselves with Jackson while the British had joined forces with Creek Indians and the Spanish, but there were only about 700 of them. A short time later, in 1817, the fort or what remained of it was once again in Spanish hands, and they promptly rebuilt it.

In July 1821, the United States took possession of both Battery de San Antonio and Fort Barrancas and immediately started to make improvements. Joseph G. Totten designed the new Fort Barrancas while Major William Henry Chase supervised the work. Both the fort and the battery were connected by an underground tunnel. Approximately 30 of the newest and most powerful cannons were mounted. Everything was meticulously done until the fort and battery along with Fort Pickens situated in nearby Santa Rosa Island were deemed suitable to defend Pensacola from both land and naval attack.

The status quo remained for nearly 40 years until January 8, 1861, more than three months before the official start of the Civil War, when a garrison of 50 federal soldiers stationed at Fort Barrancas and commanded by Lieutenant Adam J. Slemmer fired on a probing reconnaissance patrol of Florida state soldiers led by William Henry Chase, by that point a colonel. Much smaller federal forces were stationed at Fort Pickens and Fort McRee.

Knowing that Fort Pickens was easier to defend, Lieutenant Slemmer spiked his cannon by driving nails into the touchholes. For the cannons to be capable of firing, the nails would have to be drilled out, a lengthy and painstaking process. Federal forces held Fort Pickens for the duration of the Civil War.

General Braxton Bragg commanded Confederate Pensacola and stationed soldiers from Mississippi, Alabama, and Louisiana at Fort Barrancas and added sand batteries along the coast. To consolidate their position, 1,000 Confederate troops landed slightly east of Fort Pickens but were stopped. On November 22 and 23 and in early January 1862, a cannon duel erupted between Fort Barrancas and Fort McRee but shortly thereafter in May 1862, after having learned that New Orleans had fallen to Union forces, Fort Barrancas and the city of Pensacola were abandoned by the Confederacy.

Fort Barrancas is unusual in the respect that it was not designed to hold a garrison. It is basically a giant gun platform with a gallery to house foot soldiers wrapped around the inside of its base with two counterscarp galleries on two sides. There is also no parade ground. Like so many other Third System masonry forts, the advent of rifled cannons made Fort Barrancas obsolete, but it continued to serve the nation.

From 1941 to 1947, the fort was used by the U.S. Army as a signal station and a small arms range. It was deactivated in 1947. On October 9, 1960, Fort San Carlos de Barrancas was designated as a National Historic Landmark and in 1966 the Fort Barrancas Historical District was listed on the National Register of Historical Places.

Visitor Information

Fort Barrancas, 3182 Taylor Rd., Pensacola, FL 32508, nps.gov

Fort Barrancas was integrated into the Gulf Islands National Seashore managed by the U.S. National Park Service in 1971. Between 1978 and 1980, the fort underwent an extensive restoration project and was opened to the public. The fort is located inside Naval Air Station Pensacola. Access to Naval Air Station Pensacola by people who are not affiliated with the Department of Defense may be subject to Homeland Security and military force protection concerns.

CASTILLO DE SAN MARCOS
SPAIN'S JEWEL IN THEIR CROWN OF FORTS

*C*onstructed between 1672 and 1696, this massive rectangular Spanish fort on the heights overlooking the St. Johns River in St. Augustine offers expansive views of the river and the oldest continuously inhabited settlement in Florida (and in the United States, for that matter). Spanish admiral Pedro Menéndez de Avilés destroyed an existing French fort several miles to the north in 1565 and the Castillo's location was subsequently chosen.

Determined to maintain their powerful position in northern Florida, the Spanish embarked on this ambitious project that remains entirely intact complete with intricately carved smoothbore cannon whose muzzles still point down to the river as if waiting for an invading fleet that will obviously never arrive.

To safeguard Spanish interests in the New World, King Phillip II commissioned Pedro Menéndez de Avilés to dislodge the French from Florida and colonize the area for Spain. Menéndez arrived in Florida in 1565, first at what is now Cape Canaveral before traveling north to the sheltered harbor of the land he named Presidio de San Augustine.

The bastion system of fort design emerged out of the medieval castle form. Engineers lowered castle walls and placed mounds of earth in front of them, establishing ramparts capable of withstanding cannon bombardment. Moats continued to be an essential component of the defense, preventing enemy forces from scaling the sloped embankments and penetrating the fort. The round castle tower matured into the angular bastion that provided protection to contiguous walls.

Bastioned forts centered on a plaza around which immense ramparts stood. The inside of the ramparts sloped upward toward the fighting platform called the terreplein. The banquette or firing step rose above the terreplein and was protected by the parapet. On the exterior of the rampart, facing the moat, a masonry scarp retained the earthen rampart wall. On the opposite side of the moat was the counterscarp above which stood the covered way. A palisade shielded the banquette for the covered way. The glacis, an earthen bank free of foliage, sloped downward from the covered way into open country.

Seventeenth-century forts were almost always square, and the linear curtain walls extended outward at the corners into diamond-shaped bastions. Ravelins, similarly, shaped defensive structures were often constructed in front of curtain walls to provide further support to the bastion points which were most susceptible to attack. Outer defense works like counterguards and horn works, built of earth and wood and positioned in front of the fort's main body, gave additional strength to the fort. As a total defensive fortification, bastioned forts and their outer defenses gave a great deal of confidence to its residents during a siege.

Preparation for the construction of Castillo de San Marcos began in 1671 under the guidance of Ignacio Daza, a seasoned military engineer, and Lorenzo Lajones, a master of construction. Although Daza died seven months later, the work continued according to his plan. On October 2, 1672 Governor Manuel de Cendoya and other royal officials broke ground for the fort's foundation trench and several weeks later the first stone was laid. The site chosen was the location of six previous wooden forts. Local Indians, slaves, freedmen, convicts, and occasionally Spanish soldiers labored alongside skilled workers imported from Cuba.

The stone chosen for the Castillo's walls was a local stone called "coquina," meaning little shells, a type of limestone formed millions of years ago when the ocean covered Florida. The weight of the water cemented little shells together. Coquina was easy to cut when wet but became hard when dry. It was quarried from Anastasia Island across the bay from the Castillo and ferried to the construction site.

In a work area that today is the Castillo's parking lot, stonemasons produced blocks. The mortar to bind the blocks to each other was made on the construction site by baking oyster shells in kilns until they were reduced to a fine white powder called lime. The lime was then mixed with sand and fresh water to produce the mortar that still holds the Castillo together today.

Exterior View of Castillo de San Marcos, a masonry fort completed in 1695, St. Augustine, Florida
© NTZOLOV/GETTY IMAGES

About 100–150 men worked on the fort at a time. After 23 years of toil, the fort was finally completed in 1695.

The Castillo played an important role as a strategic military post in the New World and many flags have flown during its illustrious career including the Spanish (1695–1763), the British (1763–1784), the Spanish again (1784–1821), the United States (1821–1861), the Confederate States of America (1861–March 1862), and finally the United States again (1862–1900). Changes in occupation of the fort came out only through military agreements or political treaty. The Castillo was never taken by force. As a strategic deterrent, this super-fort did everything that was asked of it.

The fort defended the primary trade route to Europe and the Bahama Channel (as the Gulf Stream was then known) and it also served as Florida's territorial capitol, defending against the encroachment into the northern reaches of the Spanish Empire.

Castillo de San Marcos National Monument comprises roughly 20.48 acres. The park is north of St. Augustine's central plaza and fronts Matanzas Bay. The city itself lies on the eastern coastal plain of Florida. It is a low-lying, sandy area protected from the sea by several barrier islands.

The San Sebastian River runs west of the city and formed a natural barrier for the colony early in its history. A seawall and water battery separate the Castillo from the waters of Matanzas Bay on the fort's east side. The site of Castillo is a rolling, grassy area sprinkled with a few trees. The outer portions of the grounds are flat up to the glacis, which slopes upward toward the fort and roughly follows the contour of the moat and covered way. The park is irregular in shape with much of its western boundary following the contour of State Road A1A. The defense work runs west from the glacis to the City Gate, interrupted by Route A1A just east of the gate.

The Castillo is built around a square plaza whose sides are 230 feet long and has diamond-shaped bastions named for a different Roman Catholic saint (San Augustin, San Pablo, San Pedro, and San Carlos) protruding at each corner. The coquina walls are 30 feet high, 10 to 14 feet thick at the base, and five feet thick at the top. Originally three cisterns provided fresh water. Today there is only one.

Vaulted casements that support the wide terreplein and embrasures are situated strategically along the top of the wall. Just next to the entrance room were the guardrooms. Directly across the plaza from the entrance was the chapel.

The garrison had a nominal strength of 350 men, although that number fluctuated slightly. Deaths from yellow fever and other tropical diseases were common. In addition, rosters were sometimes inflated when deceased soldiers were surreptitiously kept on duty lists so spouses could collect benefits and pay.

Cannon were of assorted sizes and calibers, contingent on the type of ground that had to be defended. The biggest guns were on the waterfront, while the smaller calibers were consigned to the land sector that was afforded additional protection by existing rough ground.

Prior to the Castillo's completion cannon were placed only in the bastions. San Augustin (southeast bastion) protected the harbor and its entrance and St. Augustine proper, and San Pablo (northwestern bastion) guarded the land approach to the fort and the town gate. San Pedro (southwestern bastion) was inside the town limits. Its guns acted as reserve for San Pablo. San Carlos (northeastern bastion) guarded the harbor and marshland to the north.

In 1683 the Castillo was armed with 29 guns: one iron 2-pounder, one bronze 3-pounder, two 4-pounders (iron and bronze), five 5-pounders (4 iron, 1 bronze), five 7-pounders

(4 iron, 1 bronze), one bronze 8-pounder, three iron 9-pounders, two 10-pounders (iron and bronze), two 12-pounders (iron and bronze), three iron 16-pounders, one bronze 18-pounder, one bronze 40-pounder, and one iron stone mortar. Additionally, there were nearly 12 unmounted pieces (some unserviceable) including two pedreros.

The bastion San Augustin was formidably armed with one 40-pounder, one 18-pounder, two 16-pounders, two 12-pounders, one 8-pounder, one 7-pounder, one 4-pounder, and one 3-pounder. Bastion San Pablo defended itself with one 16-pounder demi cannon, one 10-pounder demiculverin, two 9-pounders, one 7-pounder demiculverin, one 7-pounder, and one 5-pounder. Bastion San Pedro was protected by one 9-pounder, two 7-pounders, two 5-pounders, and one 4-pounder. Bastion San Carlos had one 10-pounder, two 5-pounders, and one 2-pounder.

Although the bronze guns were named to signify their operational characteristics the names also had metaphorical meanings. two and 4-pounders were called falcons, 6-pounders were a.k.a. sakers (from the saker hawk), 8-, 10-, 12-pounders were known as demi-culverin (from the Latin *colubra* meaning snake), 15-, 18-, 20- and 22-pounders were named culverins, 12-pounders were referred to as third or demi-cannon, 20- and 25-pounders were a.k.a. demi-cannon while 30-, 35-, 40-, 45- and 50-pounders were identified as simply cannons although the 40-pounders were given the name double culverins or dragons. Culverins were the only guns capable of reaching the harbor sand bar, 3,000 yards away.

By 1706 the Castillo's armament had increased to 35 guns with the addition of six iron pieces ranging from 4- to 10-pounders. In 1740 the number of guns almost doubled to 65. Added were two iron and two bronze 3-pounders, four iron

4-pounders, nine iron 5-pounders, five 6-pounders, 11 8-pounders, six 15-pounders, four 18-pounders, one 24-pounder, and one 33-pounder. The greatest number of guns the Castillo ever manned was 77 in 1763 when 10 bronze 8-pounders, five iron 10-pounders, 12 iron 12-pounders, one bronze 16-pounder, seven iron 18-pounders, seven iron 24-pounders, one bronze 36-pounder, and 18 small mortars were added. In 1765 the total number of guns decreased to 63, in 1812 it was almost halved to 34 and in 1834 armament was reduced to 20 guns.

Ordnance served longer due to colonial isolation than the normal 1,200-round life of an iron piece. Common malfunctions were development of cracks around the vent or in the bore. Every now and then a muzzle blew off. Crewing these guns was not the safest thing to do and deaths were not unknown.

The most effectual assault of the Castillo ensued during the siege of 1740 in which round shot did the most harm. The heaviest British siege cannon were 18-pounders, situated over 1,000 yards from the fort. Spanish engineer Pedro Ruiz de Olano recounted that the balls did not puncture the main walls more than a foot and half thick but the parapets, being only three feet thick, suffered significant damage.

Today there are 27 pieces inside the fort and 11 outside. Because the different occupiers of the fort brought many of their own guns with them to add to the ordnance that had been left behind the collection of guns is large and eclectic. A few are original pieces including an iron 18-pounder with a range of 3.3 miles, a 24-pounder (range 3.8 miles) and two 2-pounders.

The brass guns were one of a kind, cast from wax molds that were obviously destroyed during the casting process. The attention to detail and craftsmanship is remarkable and the glyphs are somewhat analogous to medieval heraldry.

View of a sentry tower at Castillo de San Marcos.
© ROC8JAS/GETTY IMAGES

The moat, covered way, and glacis surround the Castillo on the north, west, and south sides. The moat, eight feet deep and approximately 42 feet wide, originally encircled the fort on all sides, but the east side was filled in 1842 to create a water battery. The water level could be controlled by gates in the seawall and, if needed, the moat could be drained and livestock kept in the moat to feed people inside the Castillo during an attack. A masonry wall five feet high divided the covered way from the glacis.

The water battery constitutes the east side of the Castillo between the curtain wall and the seawall. The area was infilled by the Army Corps of Engineers between 1842 and 1844 to permit the placement of guns facing the harbor. The seawall was significantly reconstructed by the Corps of Engineers between 1833 and 1844 to safeguard the fort and the city from erosion and storms and to enable the construction of the water battery.

The coquina structure is faced with granite to the high-water mark. The stuccoed, coquina hotshot furnace was built in 1844 on top of the water battery and is nine feet long and 11 feet wide. The chimney is 11 feet high.

The establishment of the seawall, water battery, and hotshot furnace was an attempt to update the Castillo and make it a contributing part of the nineteenth-century coastal defense system.

The water battery and hotshot furnace originated as a result of the Second Seminole War and national attempts to prepare the coastline in the event of naval attack. They illustrate the military thinking at the time and complement the Castillo, demonstrating the development of military engineering and technology. They also ended construction projects at the fort.

To enter the Castillo, you must cross a drawbridge and enter the ravelin. From the ravelin you must cross a second bridge before gaining access to the Castillo proper. The drawbridge from the mainland to the ravelin was raised nightly; the bridge from the ravelin to the Castillo was raised only when the Castillo was under attack.

As a provision of the Treaty of Paris that ended the Seven Years' War, Britain gained possession of Florida (and the Castillo) in 1763 and changed its name to Fort St. Marks. During the American Revolution, the fort held patriots captured by the British.

In the treaty settlement at the end of the American Revolution, Spanish troops returned to St. Augustine on July 12, 1784, and changed the name back to the Castillo. However, on July 20, 1821, due to pressures from within and without, Spain ceded Florida to the United States.

On their arrival in St. Augustine, the Americans changed to name of the Castillo to Fort Marion in honor of General Francis Marion, a Revolutionary War hero known as "the Swamp

Fox." The old storeroom was converted into prison cells and during the American Territorial Period the fort served briefly as a prison for captured Seminole warriors. Among them were Coacoochee, Blue Snake, and Osceola. During the 1870s and 1880s Kiowa, Comanche, Cheyenne, Caddo, Arapaho, and Apache Indians captured in the West were imprisoned at the fort. On May 21, 1875, 71 hostile Indians escorted by Lt. Richard H. Pratt arrived at the fort. Pratt's experience with the Indians led him to establish the Carlisle Indian Training School in Pennsylvania in 1880.

During the Civil War Fort Marion was in Union hands for most of the conflict. The fort was handed over to the Confederates in January 1861 but came back into Union hands on March 11, 1862, when the USS *Wabash*, a Union gunboat, took the city and the fort without firing a shot after realizing that Confederate forces had evacuated the area.

During the Spanish-American War in 1898, the Castillo resumed its role as a prison, holding nearly 200 court-martialed deserters from the American army. After the war the fort was decommissioned. In 1924 President Calvin Coolidge, acting under the authority of the Antiquities Act of 1906 declared Fort Marion to be a National Monument.

The fort was transferred from the War Department to the National Park Service, U.S. Department of the Interior in 1933 and in 1942 the original name, "Castillo de San Marcos" was officially restored to the installation. With the passage of the National Historic Preservation Act, Castillo de San Marcos National Monument was placed on the National Register of Historic Places in 1966. The Keeper of the Register accepted the nomination of the park as a historic district in March 1977.

Visitor Information

1 South Castillo Drive, Saint Augustine, FL 32084, (904) 829-6506

The hours: 8:45 a.m. to 5:15 p.m. every day except December 25, when the Castillo is closed. Call ahead for fees and specific hours. Everything except the gun deck is handicapped accessible. Tours are given in English and Spanish.

EAST MARTELLO BATTERY

THE SMALLEST FORT

*T*his diminutive, rectangular battery was built in Key West 1862 to protect the larger Fort Zachary Taylor and the harbor in Key West from Confederate attack. The advent of rifled cannon barrels made the brick-and-mortar building obsolete before it was completed, and it was never armed. Nevertheless, it is a quaint reminder that represents conventional military planning at the time.

Protecting Key West was a priority for the U.S. Navy when in 1822 it conducted a survey to identify the best places to establish forts. In 1836 U.S. Army Colonel Joseph Gilmore Totten and the brilliant French designer Simon Bernard drew up plans for nine forts. Budgeting restrictions reduced the number to three forts. One would be large (Fort Zachary Taylor) and the other two would be smaller (the East and West Martello Towers).

Work on the East Martello Tower (and its sister fort the West Martello Tower) was begun in the mid-1860s. Neither tower was ever involved in a battle.

Visitor Information

East Martello Battery, 3501 South Roosevelt Boulevard, Key West, FL 33040, (305) 296-3913 or (305) 294-4641

For more information contact the tower directly.

FORT BARRANCAS

THE SPANISH STRENGTHEN THEIR HOLD
ON FLORIDA'S WEST COAST

*B*uilt by the Spanish in 1797, this large, still completely intact, diamond-shaped, and well-preserved fort has magnificent views from the bluffs overlooking Pensacola Bay and the Battery San Antonio below it. The Spanish word for bluff is barrancas.

Fort Barrancus Gun Gallery is a tunnel inside the fort's walls with firing slits for the defenders to shoot from. The fort was built in 1839 to protect Pensacola bay and is now part of the Gulf Islands National Seashore
© KEITH MITCHELL/GETTY IMAGES

The fort boasts walls four feet thick and 20 feet high. An estimated six million bricks were used in its construction. There are exquisite brick archways and vaulted ceilings with views of the wide dry moat in addition to loopholes in the fort walls. The fort saw action during the War of 1812 and the Civil War.

Visitor Information

Fort Barrancas, 3182 Taylor Road, Pensacola, FL 32508, nps.gov

Check website for more information.

FORT CLINCH

THE NORTHERNMOST FORT IN FLORIDA'S COASTAL FORTIFICATIONS

*B*uilt in 1847, this large, well-preserved, Third System pentagonal fort on the Florida/Georgia border sits on a peninsula near the northernmost point of Amelia Island and to the northeast of Fernandina Beach and still stands silent sentinel as St. Mary's River slowly flows. The fort was occupied by both Confederate and Union forces during the Civil War.

Named after General Duncan Lamont Clinch who fought in the War of 1812 and played an influential role in the First and Second Seminole Wars the site was first fortified by the Spanish when they had colonies in Florida. The United States constructed the fort with inner and outer walls, corner bastions, and embrasures in the outer walls. Originally intended to hold 70 cannon, it was never fully armed.

Confederate forces seized the fort early in 1861 and used it as a safe haven for blockade runners. The advent of rifled cannon made the fort's brick walls vulnerable to attack, and in March 1862, General Robert E. Lee ordered the fort to be abandoned. Union forces reoccupied the fort in early 1862 and used it as a base of operations in the area throughout the Civil War.

In 1869 the fort was placed under caretaker status until 1898, when the U.S. Army garrisoned it during the Spanish-American

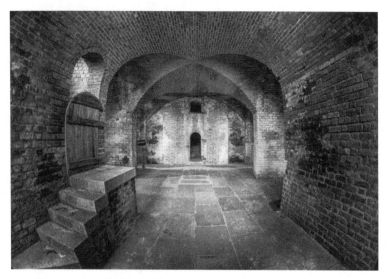

Fort Clinch. Fernandina Beach, Florida
FLORIDA MEMORY

War. In September 1869, the fort was abandoned yet again. Workers of the Civilian Conservation Corps started restoration of the fort during the Great Depression in the 1930s.

The State of Florida purchased 256 acres in 1935 that included the fort and surrounding area, and in 1938 Fort Clinch State Park was opened to the public. During World War II the fort was off limits to the public because it was used as a security and communications post. It was reopened after the war. It was placed on the National Register of Historic Places in 1972.

Visitor Information

Fort Clinch State Park, 2601 Atlantic Ave, Fernandina Beach, FL 32034, (904) 277-7274

There are two campgrounds in the park. The Amelia River one has two hot water restrooms and showers and 41 campsites in an oak hammock. The Atlantic Beach campground has one hot water restroom and shower plus 21 sites with a ramped boardwalk.

Fort Clinch on Amelia Island
© ROBERT HOLMES/GETTY IMAGES

Other activities are swimming, bicycling, picnicking, beach-combing, fishing, hiking, and wildlife viewing such as alligators, purple sandpipers, white-tailed deer, dolphins, and manatees. The park is a gateway site for the Great Florida Birding Trail. Visitors can also explore the fort's restored infirmary, laundry, barracks, kitchen, and carpenter shop.

FORT JEFFERSON
AMERICA'S GIBRALTAR

*T*his is arguably the crown jewel of all Third System fortifications. It was constructed in 1846 on 20-acre Garden Key in the Dry Tortugas, equidistant between Key West, Florida, and Havana, Cuba. The hexagonal fort is the second largest brick structure in the world (only the Great Wall of China is bigger) and can be seen from outer space. An estimated 16 million bricks were used in its construction.

Boasting an array of state-of-the-art cannons, a moat, coaling station, and remnants of barracks and a hotshot furnace Fort Jefferson was where the U.S.S. *Maine* refueled before making its ill-fated journey to Cuba. The fort also served as a listening post during the Cuban Missile Crisis and is today part of the Dry Tortugas National Park. Fort Jefferson is America's largest nineteenth-century coastal fortification with two tiers and 45-foot-high walls that are eight feet thick.

Construction began in 1825 and was completed a year later along with a 65-foot-tall, whitewashed lighthouse. The Dry Tortugas was an ideal place for such a large installation that would guard entrance to the Gulf of Mexico. The fort was instrumental in enforcing the Monroe Doctrine that was originated by President James Monroe in 1823 that stated in simple terms that any intervention by external powers in the politics of the Americas would be viewed as a potentially hostile act against the United States. In other words, North and South America were no longer open to colonization. Furthermore, the United States would not allow European countries to interfere with independent governments in the Americas. A large fleet of warships could find safe harbor in the Dry Tortugas and be protected by Fort Jefferson's cannons.

There was an inner and outer harbor where safe anchorage was afforded throughout the year. Second Lieutenant Horatio Wright supervised construction following plans drawn up by Lieutenant Montgomery C. Meigs. Chief of Engineers Joseph Totten designed the fort.

There were two-tiered casements in the six-sided fort augmented by two curtain walls that measured 325 feet long, and the other four were 477 feet long. Corner bastions contained gun rooms, gunpowder magazines, and a granite spiral staircase. Each tier of casements contained 150 guns while an additional 150 guns were situated on top of the fort itself. The guns were placed in a line of open casements facing the sea through openings called embrasures. The 13-acre parade ground held three large barracks, powder magazines, officer's quarters, a hospital, and a headquarters building.

Conditions at the fort were brutal. In the summer months the heat and humidity was almost intolerable and fresh water was at a premium. The fort received a steady supply of reinforcements. At the beginning of the Civil War, the Second U.S. Artillery Regiment led by Major Lewis Golding Arnold stationed 62 men at Fort Jefferson. On July 4, 1861, 160 soldiers (two companies) from the 6th New York Zouaves commanded by Colonel Bill Wilson arrived. Troops were rotated on a regular basis. In March 1862, the 7th New Hampshire Volunteer Infantry led by Colonel Haldimand S. Putnam relieved the Zouaves. Lieutenant Colonel Louis W. Tinelli leading the 90th New York Volunteer Infantry Regiment relieved the New Hampshire soldiers

In the nineteenth century, Fort Jefferson projected American power far out into the Gulf of Mexico. Its defensive moat was once patrolled by sharks.
© POSNOVGETTY IMAGES

in June 1862, and in turn they were relieved by the 47th Pennsylvania Infantry in December. They were replaced in March 1864 by the 110th New York Volunteer Infantry.

Because of its extremely isolated location, Fort Jefferson was an ideal place to house soldier prisoners convicted of mutinous conduct and later desertion. The first prisoners arrived in September 1861. By November 1863, the number had increased to 214 and in June 1864, there were 753 convicts at the fort along with 653 soldiers. The number of prisoners increased to 882 in November of the same year.

On July 24, 1865, perhaps the most infamous prisoner arrived. Doctor Samuel Alexander Mudd, who was a tobacco farmer and physician residing in southern Maryland, had been convicted of conspiring in the assassination of President Abraham Lincoln at Ford's Theatre along with three other individuals.

Mudd had set the broken left fibula of John Wilkes Booth after Booth shot and killed Lincoln while the president, along with his wife Mary and other dignitaries, was watching *Our American Cousin.* Moreover, Mudd was seen in the company of the other conspirators and had waited 24 hours before reporting that he was aware of the assassination. Convicted of aiding and conspiring in a murder, Mudd, along with Michael O'Laughlen, Samuel Arnold, and Edmund Spangler, was sentenced to life imprisonment by a nine-man military commission.

In September 1865, two months after he arrived, the 82nd U.S. Colored Troops replaced the 161st New York Volunteer Infantry Regiment. On the 25th of that month Mudd attempted to escape by stowing away on the transport ship *Thomas A Scott.* As a result, he and the other conspirators plus George St. Leger Grenfell were placed in an empty ground-level gun room known as the dungeon.

After an outbreak of yellow fever plagued the fort in the fall of 1867 and killed the fort's doctor, Mudd helped to quell the spread of the disease. He was pardoned by President Andrew Johnson on February 8, 1869, released from Fort Jefferson on March 8, 1869, and returned to his Maryland home on March 20, 1869. Mudd died on January 10, 1883.

When the seawall was completed in 1872, six 15-inch Rodman cannon were in place on the third or barbette tier. In total 243 Rodmans and recoilless rifles gave the fort an impressive amount of firepower.

In 1874, after being ravaged by hurricanes and repeated epidemics of yellow fever, the garrison was removed leaving only a small caretaker force at the fort. In 1889 the fort was turned over to the Marine Hospital Service and used as a quarantine station. The U.S. Navy used the fort as a coaling station. During the Cuban Missile Crisis, the Central Intelligence Agency used the fort as a listening station.

The lighthouse was decommissioned during World War I, but a naval seaplane facility and wireless station were still operational. On January 4, 1935, President Franklin D. Roosevelt designated the area as Fort Jefferson National Monument and it was listed on the National Register of Historic Places on November 10, 1970. On October 26, 1992, the Dry Tortugas and Fort Jefferson were established as a National Park.

Visitor Information

Dry Tortugas National Park, 40001 SR-9336, Homestead, FL 33034, (305) 242-7700

Fort Jefferson can be reached by seaplane, high-speed catamaran, or private vessel. Call ahead for fees. One-day excursions last 9.5 hours and include breakfast, lunch, a guided tour, and sodas and water.

If you arrive by private boat or private vessel there is an entrance fee if you want to camp in one of the six campsites. Children including international visitors under age 16 are exempt. Fees are collected through a self-service fee area on the main dock, cash or check only. You can buy a digital pass on Recreation.com. Camping is primitive. There is a public restroom but no concessions. Visitors must bring their own food, water, and shelter. There are opportunities for snorkeling but standing on or disturbing nearby reefs is not allowed. The currents can be strong. Holders of the Golden Age or Golden Access Plan receive a 50 percent discount on camping fees. Accredited educational and scientific institutions are eligible to receive free admission to the Dry Tortugas National Park. *Note:* Catamaran and seaplane prices tend to fluctuate but they rarely go down.

FORT MATANZAS

THE SMALL SISTER FORT OF THE CASTILLO DE SAN MARCOS ST. AUGUSTINE, 1742-1942

*S*ituated along the Matanzas River 14 miles south of the Castillo de San Marcos in St Augustine, this small fort built in 1742 was essentially a forward listening post and the site of a massacre on the north shore of Jean Ribault and his band of Huguenot Frenchmen, the last of the Fort Caroline colonists, by the Spanish in 1565. The Spanish word for massacre or slaughter is matanzas.

The rectangular fort had a standard garrison of seven men (one officer, four infantrymen, and two gunners) whose mission was to guard Matanzas Inlet, the southern mouth of the Matanzas River. The walls are 50 feet long on each side with a 30-foot-high tower.

This is the little fort with the big guns. Anastasia Island is a barrier island 15 miles long by anywhere from three miles to one quarter of a mile wide that is separated from the mainland by the Matanzas River. The northern end of the island is almost due east of the Castillo de San Marcos, the large, well-armed fort that protected the city of St. Augustine from naval attack. The only viable south/North Sea route is via the St. Augustine Inlet.

The less practical avenue of attack is from the south, but, because they had to sail past the Castillo, any element of surprise would be immediately lost. Ships and troops disembarking could be seen, and a fleet was always at the mercy of the often-volatile weather especially during summer months when gale force winds were not unknown.

However, assuming the Matanzas Inlet was gained, a hostile force could sail unopposed up the river and lay siege to the relatively soft underbelly of the city. The inlet itself is slightly more than one tenth of a mile or approximately 528 feet wide while the Matanzas River varies from a tenth of a mile to one mile wide.

Four years after Pedro Menéndez de Avilés landed on the Florida coast in 1565 and claimed the land for King Philip II of Spain, an unarmed, wooden watchtower was erected on the site, a relatively rectangular sand spit approximately one mile long by a third of a mile wide.

The island lies between the southern ends of Anastasia Island, which buttonhooks to the west at its southern terminus and the mainland. Most of it is snake- and alligator-infested marsh. Several species of snakes such as cottonmouths and Eastern diamondback rattlers were (and obviously still are) highly venomous. Only about one acre is solid ground. The Matanzas River is at that point quite narrow and forms a bottleneck as it merges with the inlet.

The watchtower's mission was to observe hostile ships advancing toward St. Augustine from the south, alert the settlement of the approach and deter, as best it could, enemy crafts from assaulting St. Augustine via the Matanzas River.

Also, in 1565 another story was played out at Matanzas Inlet, one that gave the fort and inlet its referential name that reveals a grisly beginning. More than 500 Frenchmen commanded by Jean Ribault left their settlement at Fort Caroline in Spanish-claimed territory near present-day Jacksonville to attack the Spanish at their new settlement of St. Augustine.

A hurricane shipwrecked and scattered the French fleet farther south. Absent of defenders, Fort Caroline was captured by Admiral Pedro Menéndez de Avilés. When the Spanish discovered 130 Frenchmen marching up the beach but blocked by the Matanzas inlet that prevented them from returning to Fort Caroline, Menéndez ordered them to surrender, give up their Protestant faith, and accept Catholicism. Having neither food nor weapons, the French surrendered but refused to renounce their faith.

Hiding most of his soldiers behind a dune, Menéndez ferried the French, hands tied behind their backs, 10 men at a time, across the inlet on September 29. They began marching toward St. Augustine, but when they reached a line Menéndez had drawn in the sand with his sword, the Spanish soldiers attacked them with sword and pike. Only 16 were spared, among them a few Catholics and four artisans needed for labor at St. Augustine.

On October 12, 11 days later, Menéndez learned that 350 more Frenchmen had also halted at the inlet. Ribault and Menéndez parleyed, and the French commander advised his men to surrender. More than half opted to flee south. The 134 who did not met the same fate as their comrades two weeks prior, although 16 men were spared including two musicians. From that time on, the inlet was called Matanzas, the Spanish word for "slaughter." Menéndez later captured those who had fled and sent them to Havana, Cuba, as prisoners.

On June 13, 1740, troops from the British colony of Georgia commanded by Governor James Oglethorpe blockaded St. Augustine Inlet in the north and began a 39-day siege of the town. Shortages of food and supplies in St. Augustine were often acute. Settlers made few attempts to farm the land around the town because of poor soil conditions and the threat of Indian attack on those who ventured too far from the settlement.

Except for produce raised in small plots around the houses, all of the colony's food, clothing, munitions, and other necessities were imported from Mexico or Havana, Cuba. Because supply shipments were often detained in Mexico and occasionally lost at sea, the residents and garrison of St. Augustine were often hungry and poorly clothed.

Oglethorpe cleverly began the siege by blocking Matanzas Inlet, thereby cutting off any southern route that Spanish ships coming to the aid of the town might take. Then he sent his other warships in through the St. Augustine Inlet in the north to attack the Castillo de San Marcos.

Spanish vessels managed to evade the blockade and resupply the town just before the onset of hurricane season. The British returned to Georgia while the Spanish, realizing the critical importance of defending the southern ingress to the Matanzas River and more than convinced that a wooden watchtower

Fort Matanzas, Spanish fort built in 1742.
© NSA DIGITAL ARCHIVE/GETTY IMAGES

was inadequate, began construction in 1740 of Fort Matanzas under orders from Governor Manuel de Montiano.

At the very least the fort armed with cannon would serve as a warning device for the Castillo that lay approximately 14-miles upriver. At best it would defend the southern approach. The fort also served as a rest stop and a place where ships going to St. Augustine could obtain navigational advice. In military parlance the fort was a forward listening post.

Construction of Fort Matanzas began in 1740 and was completed two years later. At the time, the site was still connected albeit tenuously to the mainland. During construction Spanish ships defended the fort against attack. It became a true island with the creation of the intercoastal waterway in the early 1900s.

Since construction of the fort Anastasia Island has grown (due to littoral currents that move sand along the shore from north to south, eroding northern ends of islands and depositing the sand at their southern ends) in a southern direction by about one half a mile.

The fort was small and built like a square block. As they did at the Castillo de San Marcos, the Spaniards used "coquina," Spanish for "little clam" a local resource formed millions of years ago when tiny shellfish died, and their shells bonded together and produced carbon carbonate which solidified lower layers of sunken clams in a process similar to how stalactites are formed in caves.

As luck would have it there was a nearby quarry south of the inlet on adjacent Anastasia Island, enabling the work to progress rapidly. Mortar was made by baking the ubiquitous pink, lavender, white, or yellow shells in kilns until they disintegrated into a powder called lime. The lime was then mixed with water and sand to produce the mortar.

The sides were 48 feet long and five to seven feet high. The inside of the block was solid fill, necessary to support the weight of the cannons on top, consisting of huge rocks and sand. Construction was labor and time extensive due to the long, pine logs driven deep into the mud and capped with a grillwork of square pine timbers upon which a topping of oyster shell was laid to support the stonework and stabilize the marshy terrain. A timber floor was built on top of this as a base for the cannons. A vaulted ceiling was fabricated for structural strength.

The fort could bring five guns mounted *en embrasure* to bear on the inlet; four iron 6-pounders and one iron 18-pounder. Most important, all of the guns could reach the inlet which in 1742 was less than half a mile distant.

The 6-pounders were either pasavolantes (passengers) with a point-blank range of 500 yards and a maximum range of 4,166 yards or a demisaker (little hawk) with a point-blank range of 417 yards and a maximum range of 3,750 yards. Both these guns were greatly prized because of their range and efficacy of fire. Manned by competent crews they could produce a withering barrage. The 18-pounder was well known as a ship-crippler if not outright killer.

At the rear of the gun deck was a water cistern, the island's only source of fresh water. The fort's roof caught the rain, which passed into the cistern through wooden pipes. Fort Matanzas was garrisoned by seven to 10 men who served a month's tour of duty before being relieved. The usual complement was one officer, four infantrymen or musketeers and two gunners. In times of crisis, 50 men could be shoehorned into the fort.

In the gun deck's southwest corner there is a sentry box with loopholes. The sentry could see to the south and west along and outside the walls.

The soldiers came from the Castillo de San Marcos by ship, bringing all their supplies with them. It is reasonable to assume that the men did not lack for fresh meat due to the great numbers of turtles, birds, and fish on and around the island. During periods of inactivity hunting and fishing was presumably encouraged for both dietary and morale reasons.

Accommodations were in the form of a small rectangular building that had two piggybacked rooms constructed almost as an afterthought on one side of the gun deck. One was for the regular soldiers, the other for the single officer.

Opposite the fireplace in the soldier's quarters on the gun deck was a long sleeping platform. Benches and a table completed the Spartan furnishings. The small windows in the room were for ventilation and served as gun loops for musket fire. The larger windows had shutters to keep out the rain and the clammy bite of winter winds. There was a fireplace for cooking and warmth.

The officer's quarters in an apartment above were not much better. The commander, usually a corporeal or sergeant had a desk in addition to a bed. Three loopholes in the south wall provided ventilation and the firing of muskets at attackers.

However, he and the other men as well also lived in dangerous proximity to the sometimes-volatile black powder used for the cannon that was stored in the same room and protected by only a low wall. The magazine extended down the wall and into the soldier's quarters.

The garrison slept, cooked, and ate within the confines of these cramped rooms. Fort Matanzas was for all intents and purposes a giant powder keg. One lucky shot from a well-aimed enemy cannon that hit the magazine would have blown the tiny fort and its garrison to smithereens.

Each morning at dawn a sentry on an observation deck on top of the tower would scrutinize the area for potential indications of trouble before giving the command to lower a narrow wooden ladder so the men could begin the day's activities. From his perch the sentry had an excellent view of the inlet.

At night, the ladder was pulled up. There was also a round, enclosed sentry box.

The fort saw its first action before it was even completed. On September 10, 1742, the British mounted an assault on St. Augustine through the Matanzas Inlet. When the 12-ship flotilla arrived at the inlet, cannon fire from the tiny fort drove the vastly superior British force away. The fort fired its guns only one more time. In 1810, an American gunboat attempted to capture Matanzas but was driven off by its guns.

Fort Matanzas is more than a curiosity. Acting in tandem with the much-larger Castillo de San Marcos, this diminutive installation played a major role in maintaining the military integrity of St. Augustine and keeping Spanish interests in the New World viable.

Matanzas vividly illustrates the premise that lack of physical size alone does not necessarily preclude a fort from fulfilling its assigned mission as an effective deterrent. Properly armed, garrisoned and strategically placed, Fort Matanzas effectively anchored the southern end of Matanzas Inlet.

There are two original 8-pounders at the fort, placed there during the Second Spanish Period in 1793. These guns were left behind when the U.S. government purchased Florida from Spain. There are also two reproduction 6-pounders.

In 1763 the First Treaty of Paris gave Florida to Great Britain in exchange for Cuba. Fort Matanzas was occupied by British troops to guard against a Patriot attack. The Adams-Onis Treaty, also known as the Transcontinental Treaty, the Florida Purchase Treaty or the Florida Treaty of 1821 ceded Florida to the United States and the fort was abandoned. From 1862 to 1865 Union troops manned a barge at the fort. The fort was proclaimed a National Monument in 1923 and 9 years later the fort was transferred from the War Department to the National Park Service, U.S. Department of the Interior.

Visitor Information

8635 A1A South, St. Augustine, FL 32080, (904) 471-0118, nps.gov/foma

Free ferry to the fort operates from 9:30 a.m. to 4:30 p.m. daily, weather permitting. The viewing dock, visitor center, restrooms and. six-mile boardwalk nature walk are handicapped accessible. There is ample parking. The entire site is 300 acres. There are live firings of cannons and muskets. Check for schedule.

Many species of birds such as egrets, herons, pelicans, least terns, and ospreys call the area around Fort Matanzas home as do gopher tortoises and turtles. The endangered Anastasia Island beach mouse is obviously smaller and harder to see as is the larger, also endangered but equally reclusive Eastern indigo snake, the largest nonvenomous snake in North America.

The summer months or wet season in Florida can be brutally hot and humid. Torrential afternoon rain showers are common but there are fewer people. Winter months or dry season are cooler, but the crowds are larger. It is possible to visit the fort and the Castillo in the same day. In addition, St. Augustine is a lovely town that offers many opportunities for sightseeing, fine dining, and accommodations to fit a variety of budgets.

FORT PICKENS

AMERICA'S HOME-BUILT FORT TRUMPS
SPANISH-BUILT FORT PICKENS

Construction on this pentagonal, brick-walled fort in Pensacola began in 1829 and was completed in 1933. The fort was as an answer to Fort Barrancas approximately 1.5 miles from Fort Barrancas. Fort Pickens is located at the western tip of Santa Rosa Island just offshore from the mainland and boasted over 100 cannons within and on top of its walls. It saw action during the Civil War and served as a prison after the Civil War housing the notorious Chiricahua Apache chief Geronimo.

Fort Pickens, Pensacola Beach, Florida
© ROBERT HARRIS/EYEEM GETTY IMAGES

Visitor Information

Gulf Island National Seashore, 1400 Fort Pickens Rd., Pensacola Beach, FL 32561, (850) 934-2600

Entrance fees are required and collected at the following areas of the Gulf Islands National Seashore: Fort Pickens Area, Opal Beach at the Santa Rosa Area, Okaloosa Area, Fort Barrancas Area, and Perdido Key Area.

WEST MARTELLO TOWER

TWIN SISTER OF THE EAST MARTELLO BATTERY IN KEY WEST

*L*ike its sister, this smallish fort never saw action. During the Spanish-American War it was used for quartering soldiers, storage, signaling, and as a lookout. From 1914 to 1944, it saw service as a radio station and as an antiaircraft battery. Monroe County became the owner of the towers in 1947, and in 1976 the West Tower was declared a National Historic Site by the state of Florida. It is listed on the National Register of Historic Places.

Visitor Information

1100 Atlantic Blvd., Key West, FL 33040, (305) 294-3210

The site is preserved by the Key West Garden Club. There are multiple gazebos on the property in addition to a brick path in the main courtyard that features rare, tropical plants and sculpture installations. One of the gazebos as a water lily pond and a waterfall. The tower is located on Higgs beach by the White Street Pier near stop number 10 on the Old Town Trolley tour.

FORT ZACHARY TAYLOR

KEEPING KEY WEST IN THE UNION

*A*lthough it is more than 100 years old, Fort Zachary Taylor, located in Key West, Florida, is a prime example of a Third System fort. It is also home to the largest collection of Civil War cannons that are to be found anywhere in the United States. When completed, the fort boasted a frightening and unheard total of 198 10-inch Rodmans, 8- and 10-inch Columbiads, Parrott rifles, 10-inch mortars, and howitzers. The first shipment of 50 8-inch Columbiads, along with 33,000 pounds of powder and 500 shot, arrived at the fort in late September 1854 from the Baton Rouge arsenal. The Washington arsenal sent the casement carriages for the 8-inch smoothbores and Fort Monroe contributed 1,200 8-inch shells.

These were soon followed by 24-pound flank howitzers that protected the four bastions against attempts to scale the walls. The spring of 1860 saw war clouds looming and sped the mounting of four more 8-inch Columbiads and siege mortars that faced the shore. Rapid improvements brought the total to 11 Columbiads and a number of howitzers.

Parrott rifles were next to arrive, and although the larger calibers suitable for seacoast defense were few, in part due to their tendency to burst, which made them obviously unpopular with crews and commanders alike, the lighter, field-caliber Parrotts proved to be effective weapons. One of the Parrott rifles on view at Fort Zachary Taylor bears the inscription "Rifle # 28—West Point Foundry 1861—26,910 lbs."

The fort is a trapezoid with three seaward curtains 50 feet high and 5 feet thick rising 50 feet above high water. Each curtain, containing 42 guns in three tiers (now two), was to extend approximately 225 feet in length between the bastions and the gorge or land face that was 495 feet long. Designed to hold a maximum garrison of 800 officers and enlisted men, the average garrison strength was 400.

The troop barracks, two stories high with a terreplein or barbette at the top, was built into the gorge wall and contained mortars. A large powder magazine was placed at each end of the barracks. Other facilities included noncommissioned officers' rooms, kitchens, toilets, larders, and prison cells. At the center of the gorge was the sally port, connected to the land by a 1,200-foot-long causeway that could be blown up in case of attack. Cisterns that caught and collected fresh water were located around the perimeter.

At each salient angle where the curtains met a bastion containing flank casements were planned to allow howitzer fire to sweep the walls in case of an attempt at escalade. Originally extending 1,000 feet offshore, a "floating" foundation was made up of Key West Island stone (oolitic limestone) and New England granite.

The site chosen gave the fort absolute and undisputed command of all the approaches by water into the natural harbor. It also placed the entire island of Key West under the protection of the big guns situated within and on top of the fort.

With their range of three miles, the 10-inch Rodman and Columbiad (newer guns based on the Rodman design named supposedly after the Bomford pattern of the 1812 period) cannons were more than enough to deter the Confederate navy,

Fort Zachary Taylor State Park.
© WALTER BIBIKOW/GETTY IMAGES

successfully preventing them from attempting to seize either the fort or the city of Key West.

In addition, 199 captured blockade runners sailing primarily from Havana, Cuba, and Nassau, Bahamas, were brought into Key West's harbor where Fort Taylor's almost 200 guns protected them while they were adjudicated through the federal court, which was almost continually in session.

Due in large part to the efficacy of these guns and the inadequacies of the Confederate navy, Fort Taylor was one of three forts that did not fall into rebel hands, the others being Fort Jefferson (Dry Tortugas) and Fort Pickens (Pensacola).

Rodmans were adopted as the standard seacoast weapon on February 4, 1861. These guns represented cast-iron smoothbore ordnance carried to its practical limit. Thomas J. Rodman, an Army ordnance officer, reversed the pattern of stresses accumulated in the course of cooling by solidifying his castings in opposite directions. At the time, the 15-inch Rodman was easily the most powerful service cannon in the world.

The Columbiads were produced in both 10- and 8-inch calibers and could fire either shot or shell at angles between 0 degrees and almost 40 degrees. As a result of this elevation increase the maximum range was tripled, exceeding three miles.

Plans and directions for building two Martello towers (named after the original tower in Martello Bay, Corsica, that offered stout resistance against an English fleet in 1794) were laid in August 1861. The towers were to be 1.5 and 3.5 miles from the fort. Armed with howitzers and heavy barbette guns, these appendages were intended to provide the fort with additional protection as well as exponentially extending the range of the fort's guns. Although not exactly an afterthought, they were never fully utilized or realized, and their design was particular to their circumstance of use.

Fort Zachary Taylor, Key West, Florida.
© WESTEND61/GETTY IMAGES

Construction on Fort Taylor began in 1845 and continued spasmodically for the next 21 years. Most of the artisans and mechanics were newly arrived immigrant Irish and Germans from New York while Key West slaves, contracted out by their owners did the grunt labor. Hurricanes, yellow fever, labor problems, workforce shortages, and material deficits constantly impeded progress. However, as early as 1861, the fort had a working desalination plant that produced drinking water from the sea.

The fort was also a prison. Its most well-known guest was arguably Dr. Samuel Mudd, the Maryland physician who set the broken leg of John Wilkes Booth after the deranged actor assassinated President Abraham Lincoln. Mudd was held briefly in transit at Fort Taylor before being transferred to Fort Jefferson in the Dry Tortugas, where he was to serve his life sentence.

Just before the Spanish-American War, Fort Taylor was cut down to the first tier of casements and the south curtain filled with concrete to accommodate heavy 12-inch disappearing rifles, 8-inch mortars and 15- and 36-pounder rapid-fire guns. These two new batteries, named Osceola and Adair, were planned by the Endicott Board in 1885 as part of an overall plan to modernize 13 Civil War forts.

Although many of its big guns had long since rusted or were sold for scrap, Fort Taylor continued to serve its country. Both Osceola and Adair batteries were in use during World Wars I and II. Two 12-inch model 1896 rifles were dismounted in 1942 and sent to England, where they were used to protect parts of the English Channel against an anticipated German invasion. During the Cuban Missile Crisis of 1962, radar and missiles replaced the 1896 guns.

Now a state historic site, the park occupies 87 acres, 63 of which were originally designated for the fort. There are six guns on display at the fort: two 10-inch Columbiads, one 10-inch mortar, one 8-inch Columbiad, and one Parrott rifle. In Battery Osceola three Rodmans and one Parrott rifle are partially exposed.

Excavation of the fort's guns is an ongoing project that has had great success. As funds become available, more of these precious cannons are being freed from their sandy resting places. In addition, their carriages are being treated with a new process that will eventually allow them to be displayed as well.

Visitor Information

601 Howard England Way, Key West, FL 3304, (305) 292-6713

Check for updated hours of operation and admission/parking fees. Activities include bicycling, birding (bird lists are available at the ranger station), fishing, geo-seeking, canoeing, kayaking, picnicking (tables and grills are available), scuba diving, snorkeling, swimming, and daily tours.

There are also interpretive panels, a café, shower station, ample parking, and restrooms. Beach wheelchairs are available for free.

The fort is one of the premier attractions in Key West and is well worth a visit.

INDEX OF FORTS

ABOUT THE AUTHOR

Michael Garlock is the author of numerous articles on the historic forts of Florida for periodicals such as *America's Civil War*, *North and South Magazine*, and *The Artilleryman Magazine*. His historical Roman War series *The Centurion Chronicles* is available as an ebook. He has also written about coastal fortifications in and around New York City, including Governors Island.